Grandma Sylvia's Funeral

A Interactive Play in Three Acts

Concieved by **Glenn Wein**
and **Amy Lord Blumsack**

**Created by Glenn Wein,
Amy Lord Blumsack,
The Original Company,
and *You***

A SAMUEL FRENCH ACTING EDITION

SAMUELFRENCH.COM
SAMUELFRENCH-LONDON.CO.UK

FOR PRODUCTION ENQUIRIES

UNITED STATES AND CANADA
Info@SamuelFrench.com
1-866-598-8449

UNITED KINGDOM AND EUROPE
Plays@SamuelFrench-London.co.uk
020-7255-4302

Each title is subject to availability from Samuel French, depending upon country of performance. Please be aware that *GRANDMA SYLVIA'S FUNERAL* may not be licensed by Samuel French in your territory. Professional and amateur producers should contact the nearest Samuel French office or licensing partner to verify availability.

MUSIC USE NOTE

Licensees are solely responsible for obtaining formal written permission from copyright owners to use copyrighted music in the performance of this play and are strongly cautioned to do so. If no such permission is obtained by the licensee, then the licensee must use only original music that the licensee owns and controls. Licensees are solely responsible and liable for all music clearances and shall indemnify the copyright owners of the play(s) and their licensing agent, Samuel French, against any costs, expenses, losses and liabilities arising from the use of music by licensees. Please contact the appropriate music licensing authority in your territory for the rights to any incidental music.

IMPORTANT BILLING AND CREDIT REQUIREMENTS

If you have obtained performance rights to this title, please refer to your licensing agreement for important billing and credit requirements.

GRANDMA SYLVIA'S FUNERAL officially opened in Hollywood, California on September 15, 1992. It was originally produced by Wein/Lord Productions in association with Blumsack/Debrecini/ Reilley at the Hudson Theatre with the following cast:

Gary Grossman ....Glenn Wein
Natalie Chasen ....Joanna Rush
Todd Grossman ....Barry Weinberger
Jerry Grossman ....Ron Gilbert
Ava Gerard ....Teri Kempner
Dori Grossman ....Amy Lord
skyBOY Grossman ....Richard Tanner
Mark Grossman ....Marc Kahmi
Marlena Weiss-Grossman ....Sheri Goldner
Harvey Grossman ....Richard Morof
Melissa Grossman ....Janice Mautner
Dr. Byron Franklin ....Lance Rush
Risa Iannuzzi ....Deborah Seidel
Fredo Iannuzzi ....Tom Sarpi
Dave Schildiner ....Stu Levin
Elsie Duey ....Holgie Forrester
Dr. Rachel Rosenbaum ....Lisa Diana Shapiro
Helen Krantz ....Flora Burke
Rabbi Michael Wolfe...David Ellzey
Helga Helsenrott ....Helen Siff
Vlad Helsenrott ....Steven McCarthy
————————————— Understudies —————————————
Harley Helsenrott ....Joel Marks
Hedy Helsenrott ....Simone Lazer

Directed by Glenn Wein
Sets by The Original Company
Lights by Glenn Wein
Costumes by Keith Wein
Stage managed by Laura Rohrer

GRANDMA SYLVIA'S FUNERAL officially opened in New York
City on October 9, 1994. It was produced by Dana Matthow at the
SoHo Playhouse at 15 Vandam Street with the following cast:

Gary Grossman ....Glenn Wein
Natalie Chasen ....Joanna Rush
Todd Grossman ....Barry Weinberger
Jerry Grossman ....Ron Gilbert
Ava Gerard ....Brooke Johnson
Dori Grossman ....Karen Ginsburg
skyBOY Grossman ....David Eric Rosenberg
Mark Grossman ....Marc Kamhi
Marlena Weiss-Grossman ....Sheri Goldner
Harvey Grossman ....Stanley Allan Sherman
Melissa Franklin ....Janice Mautner
Dr. Byron Franklin ....Brocton Pierce
Risa Iannuzzi ....Justine Slater
Fredo Iannuzzi ....Tom Sarpi
Dave Schildiner ....Paul Eagle
Elsie Duey ....Holgie Forrester
Dr. Rachel Rosenbaum ....Simone Lazer
Helen Krantz ....Sondra Gorney
Rabbi Michael Wolfe ....David Ellzey
Helga Helsenrott ....Helen Siff
Vlad Helsenrott ....Morgan Lavere

Directed by Glenn Wein
Sets by Leon Munier
Lights by David Lander
Costumes by Peter Janis
Stage Managed by Margaret Bodriguian

TABLE OF CONTENTS

THE COMPANY

Gary Grossman - Late 20s, nice Jewish boy, Broadway belt.

Natalie Chasen - 40s, new age earth mother to Gary and Todd.

Todd Grossman - Late 20s, cute with a cocky attitude, sexually
compulsive.

Jerry Grossman - 50s, tough ex-cop.

Ava Gerard - Early 30s, dark, post-op transsexual.

Dori Grossman - Mid 20s, Pretty, tough, Brooklyn street chic.

skyBOY Grossman - Early 30s, performance artist with no talent, out
to lunch.

Mark Grossman - Early 30s, slow "Lenny" type (*Of Mice And Men*).

Marlena Weiss-Grossman - 40s, heavy-set "bitch goddess." Make
up artist.

Harvey Grossman - 40s, nebbish "whipped" husband. Born-again Jew.

Melissa Franklin - 20s, ACLU attorney. Must play a musical
instrument.

Dr. Byron Franklin - 30s., African-American doctor.

Risa Iannuzzi - Late 20s, beautiful and pampered Jewish "Princess."

Fredo Iannuzzi - Late 20s, tough, handsome Italian.

Dave Schildiner - 70s, rich, kvetchy, kibitzer.

Elsie Duey - Early 40s, alcoholic, flamboyant Martha Mitchell type.

Dr. Rachel Rosenbaum - Early 30's, strident, strong knowledge of
psychoanalysis.

Helen Krantz - Early 70s, Vivacious yenta. Fluent Yiddish.

Rabbi Michael Wolfe - Early 30's, mild-mannered, Hebrew literate.

Helga Helsenrott - 50s, Eastern European, harried and overworked
mortuary owner.

Vlad Helsenrott - Early 30s, Dracula type. Son of Helga.

Glenn Wein dedicates this play to his mother,
Sandy Hart Wein, and Harley Alden Branitz

Amy Lord Blumsack dedicates this to her
beloved grandparents Harry and Jacqueline Grossman

Special thanks to Mark and Lori Kamhi and Flora Burke
for padding our initial $300.00 budget;
Steven Zeller for handling all of our publicity in
Los Angeles for free; the late Richard Morof for
playing Harvey so beautifully; and Dana Matthow, for
bringing Sylvia to New York where she always belonged.

ACT I

We begin outside the mortuary.

VLAD HELSENROTT is the first to arrive on the scene. After explaining that the hearse will be arriving shortly, he has the mourners (the audience) line up double file and asks them to have their memorial cards (tickets) ready. (If the audience is bunched together, they will not be able to see the coffin scene as easily.) From among the mourners, he selects four strong pallbearers to carry the casket. He writes their names down and later hands the paper to the Rabbi to read at the end of Act III when it's time to carry the coffin back out. He then proceeds to hand out invitations to Club Mortuary. He flirts with cute guys and invites them to audition as go-go boys for his new business. As he moves through the audience, he informs people of his plans to start renovating the mortuary into a nightclub as soon as the funeral is over.

HELGA HELSENROTT, Vlad's mother, arrives a few minutes later. She is extremely harried and frazzled. She greets the mourners warmly and reprimands VLAD for causing problems inside the funeral home. She runs up to the corner looking for the hearse. She does this several times before

9

*the coffin actually arrives. She apologizes to mourners for
keeping them waiting. She tells them how upset she is that
her son is turning her beautiful mortuary into a dance club.*

*RABBI MICHAEL WOLFE arrives. HELGA is surprised to
see him all grown up. She hasn't seen him since his Bar
Mitzvah. He tells her he is here to perform the service. She
says "But Rabbi Simcha Freidman always does the service." He tells her that Rabbi Freidman is in Italy having a
meeting with the Pope for world peace and that he was
asked to perform the services.*

*HELEN KRANTZ arrives right after the Rabbi. She greets
RABBI WOLFE by calling him MICHAEL. She asks where
Rabbi Freidman is. She asks about his parents, Judith and
Simcha. He tells her they are divorced and that his mother
is traveling around the country in a Winnebago. She asks
him to have his mother call her when she is in town so they
can have lunch together. HELEN then invites MICHAEL
over for lunch and tells him she will make him some lokshen
kugel (lokshn kugl).*

*HELEN greets HELGA HELSENROTT like a long lost friend.
She secretly asks HELGA if she placed SYLVIA's jewelry
in the coffin. HELGA replies that she took care of it. They
agree not to tell the Rabbi.*

*DORI GROSSMAN arrives after HELEN KRANTZ. She asks
women about their jewelry. She flirts with men on the line
until FREDO and RISA arrive.*

MARK GROSSMAN comes out from the mortuary armed with a broom and dust pan. He is kept busy by HELGA who is constantly threatening to fire him. He searches for his sister DORI. He talks to the people on line and shows baby pictures of DORI.

RISA and FREDO IANNUZZI arrive. They greet people from the back of the line. FREDO does not know many people because he married into the Grossman family. He spots DORI. She goes up to FREDO and tells him she needs to speak with him. She pulls him away and they both go across the street. As DORI pulls FREDO, he looks to see if RISA is looking. RISA is complaining to people about FREDO's philandering and asking them if she looks fat. FREDO tries to play it cool.

DORI tells FREDO that she is pregnant with his baby. FREDO tells her to keep the kid and he will build a house in Italy for her. Then they both get a little physical with each other. They notice that people are watching them and they try to return to the line inconspicuously.

RISA sees DORI and FREDO. She alerts some people to what's happening. She says "You remember what we discussed? Well he's doing it again." She's ashamed, but they are family members, after all.

RISA confronts FREDO. He explains that DORI is having some problems and he's trying to help her. He greets HELEN KRANTZ. She asks FREDO if he "took care of that thing." He responds that the garbage truck driver died peacefully in his sleep. He takes her bracelet as a payment. (FREDO is not in the Mafia, but he has well-connected friends.)

MARLENA WEISS-GROSSMAN and HARVEY GROSSMAN arrive. HARVEY has a headache and asks MARLENA is she has any Ecotrin. MARLENA asks DORI if she got the Wonder Bra and the Hooked-on-Phonics she sent her. MARLENA tells VLAD she may have work for him on her next movie as a cadaver consultant.

skyBOY (GROSSMAN) and DR. RACHEL ROSENBAUM arrive. When HELGA tries to throw him off the line because of his bohemian outfit, he tells her that he is one of SYLVIA's grandsons. He finds his brother MARK to verify this. HARVEY finds skyBOY and starts yelling at him for what he did at MELISSA and BYRON's wedding (irreverent performance art with candied yams). skyBOY also puts down his nemesis, his cousin GARY, at every opportunity. He reminds the RABBI that he will be doing a performance art piece and insists that he go first. RABBI WOLFE informs him that GARY has already taken care of the funeral arrangements and that he will be performing last. This is confirmed by the memorial cards that have been handed out to the audience which should have the schedule of events typed out and RABBI FRIEDMAN's name crossed out and WOLFE's handwritten above it. skyBOY moves five or six fun people out onto the street, gets them to hold hands in a circle and shout, "I'm letting go! I'm letting go!" Afterward he hugs all of them.

DR. RACHEL promotes her book Mommy Look At Me *and hands out business cards. (She and TODD are the only characters with business cards.) She comforts her grandfather, Uncle Dave, with shallow psychobabble such as a) The past is like your ass, it's behind you; b) I don't shrink people, I help them grow; c) I know the feelings; d) Denial is not a river in Egypt; e) One day at a time; f) Hurt people hurt people; etc.*

HELEN KRANTZ encounters HARVEY, who starts chastising her. He accuses her of stealing $2,000 from the Hadassah. She is aghast at his accusations and insists she didn't steal anything. She only borrowed to buy music for the chorus. He also accuses her of sleeping with all the Grossman men after their Bar Mitzvah and that now she has extended this service to the entire Hebrew school near the Hadassah Sisters office. She insists that she was only doing her community duty by teaching the boys safe sex. She bawls Harvey out for making these accusations in front of all the mourners. He admonishes her to pay back the money.

ELSIE DUEY and DAVE SCHILDINER arrive. ELSIE has obviously had a few drinks. She is deeply interested in what people are wearing and she shamelessly brandishes her jewelry. She loudly informs the audience that she wants DAVE to open an accessory boutique for her. She mentions that she is there to support DAVE, but that she doesn't think SYLVIA was that fond of her because before she came along, Uncle Dave used to pay for all of SYLVIA's cruises, etc. When ELSIE came into the picture, it cut into SYLVIA's action a bit.

DAVE mixes with the mourners. He thanks BYRON for all the help he gave SYLVIA at the hospital after she was struck by the garbage truck. He asks RACHEL about her parents Marsha and Michael. He asks the RABBI why he is here in stead of RABBI FREIDMAN, and also about the particulars of the eulogy.

Outside of this one instance, nobody should say SYLVIA was hit by a garbage truck. It should be a surprise when the RABBI mentions this at the top of the eulogy. If anyone asks, just say, "She was in a horrible accident."

JERRY GROSSMAN and NATALIE CHASEN arrive. HELGA tells them that the hearse broke down on the Belt Parkway and that TODD and GARY went with a taxi to pick up the coffin. HELEN KRANTZ eavesdrops and shrieks, "Oy gevalt!" JERRY goes to a public payphone and attempts to call his son TODD. The cast spreads the news of the hearse breaking down through the line of mourners.

MARLENA picks on NATALIE whenever she can. She reminds her that she's not in the family. She tells other people that NATALIE worked as a hooker for both the Mayflower Madam and Heidi Fleiss and that JERRY's poor wife SANDY is locked up at the Pembrook Pines Mental Institution in South Florida.

MELISSA and DR. BYRON FRANKLIN arrive. MELISSA is carrying her violin (or other instrument) in its case. MELISSA is very distraught and BYRON comforts her.

*A taxi cab arrives, driving past the line of mourners. The pace
of events achieves fairly rapid succession. TODD is in the
front seat and GARY is in the trunk, hood up, holding the
coffin. HELGA runs after the cab, waving a hanky, and
tells it to back up. When the taxi slowly reverses, NATALIE
moves to the side of the taxi, grabs GARY's hands, and
bounces backward in tiny lady-like steps. The cab stops at
mid-point of the mourner line. VLAD and the RABBI position the four pallbearers near the taxi so they will be unexpectedly in the right place when the coffin falls.*

*Both TODD and GARY leave the taxi. GARY scolds his father
for not returning his call that morning. NATALIE hugs both
TODD and GARY. MARK wants to help carry the coffin
and both brothers discourage him. GARY tells DORI to get
her brother off of the coffin. MARK throws himself on the
ground screaming, "I WANT TO HELP WITH THE COF-
FIN! I WANT TO HELP WITH THE COFFIN!" DORI reprimands him by kicking him on the ground with her mules
and swinging her shoulder bag at him. GARY tells DORI
to take care of her brother because he doesn't want him to
get hurt. MARK gets more hysterical. GARY gives in and
brings MARK to the front of the coffin so that he can help
lift it.*

*GARY carries one side of the coffin and TODD carries the
other. MARLENA barks out orders to MARK, directing the
whole production, "Bend your knees!" Mark bends his
knees too much and the coffin is accidentally dropped on
top of him.*

This sight upsets DAVE, and he goes inside. skyBOY blames GARY for dropping the coffin. DR. BYRON checks MARK over to make sure that he is okay. NATALIE hugs MARK (who is infatuated with her) and also tries to see that he has not been injured. MARK pushes her onto a parked car or against a tree and humps her. NATALIE screams at least four times, "My tubes! My tubes!" After BYRON pulls MARK off of NATALIE, she worries to the audience that her fallopian tubes were untied to conceive JERRY's daughter. "How am I supposed to get pregnant now?" she cries.

HARVEY and JERRY come to help with the casket. HARVEY, JERRY, and the four pallbearers from the audience take the casket into the chapel up the steps. Once HARVEY is helping, MARLENA says to put GRANDMA down, that she is dead weight. HARVEY gets mad at her and yells, "The general! Cecille B. DeMother! The Führer! The senator!" MARLENA yells back, "Is your yarmulke on too tight?"

The men bring the casket to the stand onstage. MARK guards the coffin. JERRY and HARVEY escort the four pallbearers back outside to their companions.

Still outside, GARY asks TODD to stay with him. TODD ignores GARY and starts hitting on all the women. GARY gets back in the cab and asks the cabbie to reverse until they get to TODD. He finds TODD at the back of the line, gets out of the cab, and orders him to get in the taxi. TODD refuses. (GARY hugs an old Jewish lady and says, "You look good kinahorrah.") TODD and GARY go to the cab, TODD helps GARY get inside, and then slams the door on him. The cab drives off. TODD goes back to flirting with women.

JERRY finds GARY and walks back to the mortuary with him. GARY thanks the RABBI for his help on the phone last night. GARY asks VLAD if there will be a hearse to pick up the casket after the funeral. When VLAD responds half-heartedly, JERRY tells him, "There better be a hearse here with the motor running when we leave."

HELGA goes into the chapel and starts handing out the yarmulkes. VLAD comes in to check on the coffin and make sure everything is all right. JERRY finds GARY in the hall-way and he takes him to the bathroom to cry. GARY repri-mands him for not helping with anything.

If a character's name is not mentioned in a beat, then they should be on the line with the rest of the audience, shmoozing.

HELEN goes to DAVE, and after offering sympathy on the loss of his sister, asks him for a loan of $2,000 to pay back the Hadassah. DAVE is shocked that she is asking him for money at a funeral. She slinks away, but not before she tells his girlfriend ELSIE DUEY about needing the money. ELSIE offers to get it for her afterwards.

Meanwhile the audience is greeting UNCLE DAVE, ELSIE, NATALIE, MARLENA, HARVEY, and the rest of the family in the chapel. NATALIE recognizes friends from her "Aromatherapy" and "Sacred Sexuality Workshops." MARLENA is name-dropping and insulting HARVEY and NATALIE. (Ex: "Harvey, you see how nice _____ trims

his beard? Why does your face have to look like a vagina?")
HARVEY tries to rationalize why he didn't visit his mother in
the hospital. MARLENA tells him not to overreact because
they would be in town soon anyway and GARY is always
so dramatic that they assumed Sylvia probably suffered only
a scrape from the accident. UNCLE DAVE gets nostalgic
for his breakfasts with Sylvia at the Rascal House on Miami
Beach. ELSIE admires everyone's eccentric outfits and tries to
bring a positive Irish wake attitude to the proceedings.

DORI approaches HELEN and admires her jewelry. DORI
says it looks like her grandmother's. HELEN insists that
Sylvia bought the same pieces. DORI pressures HELEN to
assure her that Sylvia's favorite jewelry is inside the coffin.
HELEN tells the mourners around her that she doesn't trust
DORI.

When about 65% of the audience is inside and seated,
MARLENA goes to the casket and opens it. The audience
cannot see inside the coffin. The audience can see a tag on
the coffin that reads: $499 as is. To MARLENA's horror,
Sylvia's makeup is done in all the wrong colors. She has
MARK help her redo the makeup. The dialogue is as fol-
lows:

MARLENA. *(At bottom of stairs.)* Marky, can you help
your Aunt Marlena up the stairs, honey? *(MARKY helps her
up and gives her a kiss and a hug.)* Marky open up the coffin.
I want to see how Grandma looks. *(MARKY opens up the coffin.)* Oh my G-d! What have they done to her? I have to fix her
up ... *(MARLENA goes into her bag to get her blush, gives a*

look at Grandma, as if to say "How am I gonna do this?")
Marky honey, can you pull out Grandma's teeth?

*(MARK struggles because of rigor mortis. He pulls out
Grandma's teeth.)*

MARK. Wow!
MARLENA. You see that? Look what happened to
Grandma. *(MARK sucks in cheeks to mimic what Grandma
looks like. MARLENA applies blush.)* She needs lipstick.
Marky go like this—*(MARLENA puts fingers to her cheeks to
show him how pucker Grandma's lips. MARK puckers his own
lips.)* No! To Grandma silly!
MARK. Oh...
MARLENA. Ooh, I got all fah-smitched. *(MARLENA
reaches into her bag for a tissue.)* Marky stick out your tongue.
*(MARLENA wipes tissue on MARK's tongue and cleans
Grandma's mouth. This happens three times. Then she reap-
plies lipstick.)* Marky, can you make Grandma move her lips?
MARK. *(Trying to.)* Her lips ain't moving Aunt Marlena...
MARLENA. Okay, we'll blot. *(MARLENA takes out a tissue that has lipstick blot already on it, puts it next to Grandma's
mouth.)* Okay, open her mouth. Close it, again. *(MARK opens
and closes Grandma's mouth. MARLENA pulls out tissue. She
displays the blot to MARK.)* You see that, that's a blot.
MARK. Wow!
MARLENA. Okay, let me fix up her hair.

(MARLENA closes coffin on MARK's finger.)

MARK. My finger! Kiss it Aunt Marlena! Make it better.

MARLENA. I'll do better... *(MARLENA places his hand on her breasts and rubs it.)* Is that better? *(When Aunt MARLENA lets go of MARK's hand, MARK reaches out with the other one for Aunt MARLENA to put on her breast. MARLENA laughs.)* You didn't hurt that one, you little monkey!

(MARLENA walks off the stage. On her way back through the crowd, she tells people, "They had her in peach and pink and she shouldn't be in corals."

JERRY and GARY approach the coffin to pay their respects. GARY throws himself across the coffin spread-eagle, and cries hysterically. skyBOY ridicules GARY's outburst. NATALIE strokes GARY's tush, and asks the front row, "Doesn't he have Grandpa Harry's buns?" Then she tells them, "This is the only thing that will calm him down." [Rubbing his buns.] She approaches them and tells the people in the front row that GARY was the favorite grandson. MARK shouts that he was the favorite grandson, and NATALIE says, "These were her two favorite grandsons." NATALIE spritzes GARY's face with the Evian facial mist. They leave the stage and she escorts a teary eyed GARY to the row in front of HELEN KRANTZ. HELEN apologizes that she's sitting next to HELGA instead of him, but she was sort of roped into it. GARY asks HELEN and everyone in the surrounding area if they've seen Abe yet. He asks JERRY if he's going to be sitting shiva at Grandma's apartment. JERRY says he wants to stay with NATALIE at a hotel "tonight." GARY asks an audience member, "Am I right or wrong? When you're sitting shiva, you're not allowed to make phone calls?" GARY talks JERRY into staying at

Grandma's apartment for the duration of the seven-day shiva. NATALIE supports GARY.

DR. RACHEL goes up onstage. MARK comes over and hugs her. His hands travel slowly down to her butt. She politely removes his hands. She then goes over to the casket and pays her respects. She is onstage for no more than one minute.

DORI goes over to the coffin. When she thinks no one is paying attention she opens it and takes out the jewelry. She slams the lid shut. [This needs to be heard by the entire house.] She puts the pearl necklaces and charm bracelets on. TODD sees this and runs onstage.)

TODD. What the hell are you doing?

DORI. She's my Grandma too!

TODD. Bitch! *(He runs to GARY and JERRY.)* Gary! Dori's taking all of the jewelry off Grandma's dead body!

GARY. *(To TODD.)* Why don't you do something? Why are you standing there like an ox?

JERRY. Come here, Dori.

(JERRY runs to DORI. DORI and JERRY struggle and she breaks away from him. She runs up the aisle and TODD catches her.)

DORI. *(Emotional build with line.)* Don't you know Jews aren't supposed to be buried with their jewelry on?

JERRY. What's she talking about?

DORI. You better watch out, Uncle Jerry, because I know something about you!

JERRY. *You* better watch out!

HELEN. Oh my G-d! A fight at a funeral!

GARY. Throw her out! That's not the jewelry, that's the chach-ke-ree-uh!

VLAD takes DORI to the back of the chapel and gives her some cocaine to placate her.

AUNT MARLENA tells the back row that that particular law doesn't apply to Jews with homes in New York and Miami Beach. She then joins the RABBI with the rest of the immediate family.

skyBOY gets DORI to go back to her seat. GARY tells skyBOY that he doesn't want DORI here. skyBOY tells GARY that she was their grandmother too. GARY tells skyBOY that they are not getting the charms off of Grandma's bracelet with their names and profiles. skyBOY says that he will just have to go to Caldor's and get some himself.

DR. RACHEL is the last person to sit down. She is having a mild hissy fit over being assigned a seat all the way in the back.

After HELGA gets everyone seated, she asks GARY if she can start. He turns to HELEN, who says they can't wait for Abe any longer. GARY nods dramatically to go ahead. HELGA puts a yarmulke on TODD's head. GARY tells TODD, "Put the yarmulke on! You're Jewish. Face it." HELGA tells TODD if he takes it off again she's going to get "the staple gun." HELGA scurries to the stage.

END OF ACT I

ACT II

"The Eulogy"

HELGA. May I have your attention please? May I have your attention please!

VLAD. *(Loudly from the back of the chapel.)* Mother!

HELGA. Vladimir! *(She gives him a pleading look. Beat.)* Welcome to the Helsenrott Funeral Home. For those of you who don't already know, my name is Helga Helsenrott, and I own and run these mortuaries with my son *(Pause.)* Vlad. *(MARK applauds for VLAD. VLAD takes a bow from the back of the house facing the audience.)* At this time I would like to ask you, out of respect for the Rabbi and the immediate family, you must now turn off all recording devices. Turn off all your telephones, anything that goes beep, beep, beep. *(To a female audience member.)* Turn off all your vibrators, sweetheart. Which reminds me, I'd like to point out that the terlits are downstairs in the Helsenrott Vestibule, if you should need them. *(To audience member.)* Don't look so surprised, sweetheart, you may need it. Now we are finally ready to begin the services for my dear friend and Hadassah shvester, Sylvia Schildiner Grossman.

HELEN KRANTZ. Helga! I'm saving a seat for you!

23

(HELGA makes her way to the seat next to HELEN KRANTZ.)

VLAD. Mother, you sit up front with me.

(HELGA sits next to HELEN.)

HELEN KRANTZ. No, you promised to sit with me. So sit.

VLAD. MOTHER!

HELEN KRANTZ. Sit Helga.

HELGA. *(She stands.)* She was my friend too. So today I'm sitting here!

HELEN KRANTZ. Good gezogt!

VLAD. This is not over.

GARY. *(Aside.)* Please stop it.

HELGA. Gey! Gey-gey-gey!

VLAD. Gay... gay... gay! They all know I'm gay! *(Once onstage, VLAD indicates to MARK to go get the RABBI. MARK exits. VLAD crosses to his chair and sits down.)* Mama, you put your tuchus here now!

(VLAD points for his mother to sit on a cushion next to his feet.)

HELGA. What are you doing now Mr. Smartypants? *(VLAD exaggerates his mug.)* And don't give me none of your funny looks. Okay! That's it! You know what I'm going to do? I'm going to take off my glasses *(She does.)* so I don't have to see you no more! Poof! You disappear! You're gone!

*(MARK is the first to emerge and he takes his seat in the audi-
ence. The RABBI follows behind MARK. Behind him are
UNCLE DAVE with cigar in mouth, ELSIE, JERRY,
NATALIE, MARLENA, and HARVEY.)*

MARLENA. *(To JERRY.)* What are you pushing for? You
want to sleep with her, then sit with her! *(To audience.)* It
she's good enough to shtup, she should be good enough to sit
with.

*(The immediate family takes seats, MARLENA and HARVEY
on one bench and JERRY, NATALIE, ELSIE, and DAVE
scrunched up on the other. The RABBI has them stand up
and then sit down.)*

HELGA. *(Whispering loudly to get the RABBI's attention.)*
Rabbi! Michael!
GARY. *(To HELGA.)* You don't tell a RABBI what to do.

*(The RABBI turns around to the mourners and realizes that
they have been sitting there all along. He turns around to
the immediate family to have them stand up again and then
has all the mourners stand up as well.)*

ELSIE. We just did this.
RABBI. Will the mourners please rise?

*(Everyone rises. With a calm self-assurance, RABBI silently
flips his hands over to indicate that everyone should sit
down.)*

DAVE. We sit down, we stand up. We stand up, we sit down. It's a meshugas.

ELSIE. Dave honey, stop complaining.

DAVE. Who's complaining?

ELSIE. You are.

DAVE. I'm not complaining.

ELSIE. You are.

RABBI. Please, Dave, I'm sorry. Let me apologize to all of you. This is my very first funeral service. As a fourth year student at Hebrew Union College, I'm honored to be chosen to eulogize such a wonderful woman. I'm happy to say I knew Mrs. Grossman personally. She was at my Bar Mitzvah. In fact it was there she told me that I would become a Rabbi. And I said, "No," but she was right. So to honor her today I wore my Bar Mitzvah jacket. *(Jacket is several sizes too small.)* And now the service for our beloved Sylvia Schildiner Grossman. *(singing)* Esah Anai El Heharim. Meh Ayin Yavoh Esree. Esree Meheem Adonai. Oseh Shamayin. *(He loses the melody and performs the Va aretz like a little boy with a tinker piano, lost and devoid of emotion.)* Va-a-a-a-a-aretz. *(MARLENA starts drinking from a water bottle in a net holder with a shoulder strap.)* I raise my eyes to the mountains from whence comes my help. My life comes from Adonai, Creator of all Heaven and Earth. Sylvia Schildiner Grossman came to us from the heavens, passed through our lives, *(Awkwardly.)* was hit by a garbage truck, *(Beat.)* and has now returned to the infinite.

DAVE. Why is the box closed? She was beautiful in life, she'll be beautiful in death. It should be open!

(DAVE runs over to the casket and tries to open it. JERRY

attempts to stop him.)

MARLENA. Uncle Dave—bad make-up. She was a winter person and they put her in summer colors.

(JERRY and UNCLE DAVE return to their seats.)

ELSIE. Don't upset yourself. You had one heart attack already.

NATALIE. I'll close your chakras.

(NATALIE gets up and using the ceramic hand she wears around her neck she tells DAVE to breathe in while she cleanses his head chakra, his heart chakra, and then his sexual chakra. When she waves the hand over DAVE's groin DAVE gets nervous and protectively covers himself and ELSIE gets upset. NATALIE returns to her seat on the RABBI's line "sense of loss" and kicks her leg up in the air like a Rockette, which is an action that happens every time she sits down. Her leg crosses over JERRY's leg.)

RABBI. We are gathered today as family and friends united in our sense of loss. *(Pause for reaction to NATALIE's kick.)* And it is a sense of great loss, because Sylvia was a great woman.

GARY. *(Deeply upset.)* Amen.

RABBI. *(RABBI nods his head in sympathy.)* She touched each of our lives in a unique and memorable way. As a wife, a mother, a sister, friend, a grandmother, and a leader of the Jewish community. So individually and collectively, we have a certain sense of emptiness, a profound sense of grief, as if a part of our own soul has been ripped away. But amidst this pain, we also acknowledge that we are held in the loving hands of G-d. And we are reminded of this by the words of the 23rd Psalm. So at this time I would like to call forward Jerry and Harvey, Sylvia's attending sons, to join me now in reading the 23rd verse of Psalms.

(JERRY kisses NATALIE on the lips a little too long. HARVEY attempts to copy his brother and MARLENA flicks his kiss away with her claw-like nails. As the men approach the bima MARLENA brushes off HARVEY's behind.)

MARLENA. You've got shmutz all over the back of your jacket.

RABBI. And, I want to be correct about this. Jerry, you're the middle son and Harvey you're the youngest. *(They nod in approval. If an audience member asks where the oldest Stanley is, the RABBI should say he's at the cemetery taking care of the plot.)* Please join us as we read the 23rd Psalm, which begins, "The lord is my shepherd." Please join with a full voice. Jerry, you'll begin on this page.

(JERRY nervously gropes for his glasses in his jacket pocket. When he is unable to find them, her turns to NATALIE for help.)

NATALIE. *(Commenting while searching in vain for his glasses in her little bag.)* I've got Aunt Ceil's purse.

(JERRY respectfully pulls the RABBI's glasses off his face. The RABBI accidentally closes the Holy book. JERRY doesn't know where to begin. The RABBI blindly runs his hand

along the bima looking for the book. JERRY hands the
glasses back to the RABBI in order to find the page. The
RABBI hands JERRY back both the opened book and the
glasses. This needs to happen quickly. The RABBI raises
his arms as if he's about to begin. Then he's interrupted by
JERRY.)

JERRY. In Hebrew?
RABBI. No, In English, please, so we can all follow along.

(UNCLE DAVE reads the following louder and faster than
everyone else. The RABBI walks through the audience and
coaxes people to join in.)

JERRY and ALL. "The Lord is my shepherd. I shall not
want. He maketh me to lie down in green pastures. He leadeth
me beside still waters. He restoreth my soul. He guideth me in
straight paths."
ELSIE. *(To DAVE.)* Slow down.

(JERRY stops UNCLE DAVE and tries to start again.)

GARY. *(To skyBOY.)*   skyBOY. *(To GARY.)*
Straight paths!   Gay paths!

(skyBOY blows GARY a contemptuous kiss.)

ELSIE. Watch Jerry.

(JERRY conducts with his arm for UNCLE DAVE to join him
in unison.)

JERRY and ALL. "Yea, though I walk through the valley of the shadow of death, I will fear no evil, for Thou art with me. Thy rod and Thy staff they comfort me."

RABBI. Harvey, if you'll continue now please. We'll begin with "Thou preparest."

(HARVEY starts to daven and read in Hebrew. Jerry stops him after three davens.)

JERRY. Harv! In English.

(HARVEY looks up at JERRY stupefied.)

MARLENA. *(She is disgusted and spits out to her friends in the audience.)* Super Jew!

HARVEY and ALL. "Thou preparest a table before me in the presence of mine enemies. Thou anointest my head with oil. My cup runneth over. Surely goodness and mercy shall follow me all the days of my life. And I shall dwell in the house of the Lord forever."

RABBI. Let us all now say Amen.

(As HARVEY and JERRY return to their seats, MARLENA yells at her husband.)

MARLENA. Mr. Born Again Jew! Before, you couldn't put two words together in Hebrew! All of a sudden you grow a beard and you're fluent?!

(If actor doesn't have a beard, then HARVEY should daven a little too excitedly and MARLENA should say, "You almost

*davened yourself into a coma." or "You almost gave your-
self whiplash, davening like that!")*

RABBI. In Brighton Beach, Brooklyn in 1916...

DAVE. What 1916?

RABBI. Let me just clarify here. I spoke with Dave last
night on the phone and I spoke with Gary and Helen. They
each gave me the birth date of Sylvia. But there's a problem.
The dates are all different. As far as I can gather, Sylvia, as
she approached the age of 65 added a few years so she could
get the senior citizen discount. And then as she got older, we
all know she got younger. So, who knows? So, for all intents
and purposes, today we'll say with all due respect, the year
was 1916.

DAVE. It was 19 and 12! I should know!

RABBI. She grew up in Brooklyn. She met her husband,
Harry Grossman, at the Paramount Theater. They were married on Christmas Day in 1937. And within ten years they had
three wonderful boys. Stanley, the asparagus king, may he
live and be well with this year's asparagus crop in Poestinkill,
New York. Jerry—

(The door slams loudly as AVA GERARD enters.)

ELSIE. *(Aside.)* Who's that?

HELEN KRANTZ. Oh my G-d!

DAVE. ABEraham! Isaac and Jacob.

RABBI. ... who Sylvia hoped would lead a congregation
as a cantor, began his studies in New York—

AVA. Excuse me, Rabbi, I usually *come* much more quickly.

GARY. What?

(AVA takes her seat, and the RABBI starts speaking again.)

RABBI. *(To AVA.)* It's okay. It's all right. Even if you're late. It's just good that you could com—*be* here. Jerry began his studies to become a cantor, but then he became a New York City policeman and now resides in Miami with his successful private detective agency.

JERRY. Security company.

RABBI. Excuse me, his security company. But it was Harvey who, after years of secular living, renews his commitment to our people. *(ELSIE starts to squirm.)* With his senior citizen volunteer work at the Westside Jewish Community Center in Los Angeles. His work there brought Sylvia so much comfort.

DAVE. *Now* you gotta pee?

ELSIE. Yeah, can I go?

DAVE. Go!

ELSIE. *(Gets up, very wobbly.)* Sorry Reverend.

DAVE. Reverend?!

ELSIE. I mean Rabbi.

(ELSIE weaves her way down the aisle paying compliments to certain audience members on the aisle as she exits. "He's kind of cute for a Rabbi". "When are we going to Atlantic City?" "When ya gotta go you gotta go." "That's a nice sweater." HELGA follows her out quietly, worrying that she shouldn't fall and muttering about her accident insurance. As ELSIE is leaving the chapel she should start singing a frivolous song, such as, "Everyone Is Beautiful [In Their Own Way].")

RABBI. Harvey's work at the Westside Jewish Community Center in Los Angeles brought Sylvia great comfort. Because, next to her love of you, her mishpokhe, was her love for the Jewish people. So, she took the mitzvah of providing for her zindelekh a Jewish education very seriously. Each of the boys were Bar Mitzvahed and they each went to Jewish summer camp in the Catskills, where Sylvia toiled in the kitchen so that her boys could study Torah *(Pronounced Toy-rah.)*. Now her husband Harry ... Harry was a rather bohemian musician.

DAVE. He was a bum!

RABBI. He was a rather frugal man.

DAVE. Frugal! He was a schnorrer!

(NATALIE shushes him. He puts his hand on her knee. He taps her knee three times to get the audience's attention. Then his hand slowly climbs up the inside of her left leg toward the promised land.)

RABBI. And this situation gave Sylvia the challenge of providing for her family both educationally and monetarily. She held the family together. She became the backbone of this family and she held this family together *all the way up...*

(NATALIE takes DAVE's hand off her leg. She puts the ceramic hand hanging from her neck on her crossed knee for protection. JERRY places NATALIE's purse between her and DAVE. DAVE gives a shrug to the audience [with the cigar in his mouth] as if to say, "Can you blame me?")

RABBI. *(Continues.)* ... all the way up until the day of her passing. One of the ways she would do this would be with her marvelous meals. Her incredible menus. I'm sure many of you remember, and speak up if you remember her chicken fricassee—

GARY. The best! *(Aside.)* Remember the gravy with the corn bread?

skyBOY. *(Aside.)* There were too many neck bones.

RABBI. Some of you, I'm sure more of you remember her roast beef and kasha varnishkes.

GARY. *(Aside.)* She didn't defrost it. She threw it in the oven frozen.

RABBI. Her potato latkes!

RACHEL. *(Aside.)* They gave me gas.

RABBI. There are other dishes being called out, but we'll talk more about it at shiva. But I remember one person specifically who will never ever forget her unreal honey cake. Right Harvey?

(HARVEY moans enthusiastically and caps it off with three kisses to the sky. MARLENA copies his reaction to shame him.)

MARLENA. What is that all about? You sound like you're having an orgasm! Just pipe down! You're embarrassing me.

(MARLENA looks down and sees that HARVEY is wearing two different socks. She tells him to hide his feet.)

RABBI. But it was at these dinners when the issues of the day would be discussed. For instance, in the late Sixties they fought over whether or not to vote for Nixon.

(skyBOY hisses.)

DAVE. *(To skyBOY.)* He was a good friend to Israel!

RABBI. Please, please. They discussed who had or had not read *Valley of the Dolls.*

HELEN KRANTZ. Oh I loved that book!

GARY. *(Softly to HELEN.)* Shah still.

RABBI. But in New York in the later 40s and early 50s, the times were hard for the Grossman family. And it was this time that give birth to the Hadassah Sisters, which Sylvia formed with her dear friend Helen Krantz from Middle Village, Queens. Stand up so everyone can pay their respects. Now the Hadassah Sisters—

HELEN KRANTZ. *(Stands.)* Excuse me Rabbi, it's the Hadassah Girls!

RABBI. I'm sorry. The Hadassah Girls...

skyBOY. *(Aside.)* They ain't girls no more.

HELEN KRANTZ. Thank you.

RABBI. ... started out in Sylvia's lanai with only six of Sylvia's and Helen's friends from their weekly card game.

DAVE. And 6,000 dollars of my money.

RABBI. And now the Hadassah Girls is a 200-voiced augmented choir with which Sylvia soloed last Shavous. Quite an accomplishment!

RACHEL. *(Comment.)* She was tone deaf.

RABBI. But the New York winters were to become more harsh. And our sages taught, "Mishaneh Makum Mishaneh Mazal. Change your place, thus you change your luck." So in 1951, Sylvia changed her place and moved her family from Middle Village, Queens, to suburban Sheepshead Bay, Brooklyn, where there was better heat. There she lived happily with her Harry until 1978, when her life changed with Harry's unfortunate passing.

DAVE. Aleva sholem.

RABBI. Zichrono livracha. May his memory be for a blessing. *(RABBI motions to audience to join him in saying Amen.)* Amen. Sylvia's life would never be the same. She was able to pursue her lifelong fascination with cruising on ocean liners. *(ELSIE comes down aisle spraying perfume all over herself. She has toilet paper stuck to the bottom of her shoe. HELGA runs after her bent over, trying to pull the toilet paper off.)* And she became, during this time, the flamboyant redhead that we all remember on this solemn day. Sylvia loved to travel, and every year she returned to Israel, but on one condition: that she stay at the King David, and go to Angetti for the Dead Sea Mud Baths.

(ELSIE falls on the floor. RABBI hands HELGA the toilet paper. When she moves back to her seat, MARK reaches out into the aisle and tries to grab the toilet paper from her. She slaps his hand and sits back down next to HELEN. HELEN whispers to HELGA to throw the paper beneath her seat. DAVE, JERRY, and HARVEY rush to pick ELSIE up. They react to her putting on too much perfume. The bottle rolls out of her purse. HARVEY picks it up and gives it to DAVE.)

ELSIE. Nobody noticed.

DAVE. You stink! What did you do?

ELSIE. I just freshened up.

DAVE. Did you take a bath in the stuff?

ELSIE. It's Natalie's love oil.

NATALIE. *(With wide-eyed innocence.)* It's the Aura of Clitoris.

(DAVE sits down one step away from ELSIE. The RABBI starts to sneeze. MARLENA takes out a tissue and wipes HARVEY's fingertips off because he is sniffing them. MARLENA takes a portable fan out and fans the scent away from her. She turns the fan between HARVEY's legs to cool him down. She motions for him to cover himself with his jacket.)

RABBI. Elsie, you took quite a fall. Are you okay?

ELSIE. I just hurt my pride.

RABBI. Well Baruch Hashem ... *(Pause.)* ... you're okay. Now, when Sylvia returned from Israel she was always invigorated...

ELSIE. Did anybody see a thumbnail?

(HELGA looks into the aisle for it. DAVE retrieves it for ELSIE, but he is still annoyed.)

RABBI. ... when she came back. She even began a brief acting career, thanks to Aunt Marlena's talents as a make-up artist in the TV and film industry. Now as I've said, change your place, thus you change your luck. Well, in this case, since Sylvia's youngest son Harvey changed wives and married Marlena, Sylvia's luck recently blossomed with a cameo appearance in *The Bridges of Madison County.* (*The name of the movie and the role played are topical.)*

MARLENA. She was the toll booth collector on the bridge. *(Beat.)* They cut it though. *(Beat.)* It happens.

RABBI. But amidst her busy and active life she always had time for her pride and her joy, her grandchildren. Stanley's children: Stuart—

(The RABBI crosses to each of the grandchildren and shakes their hands.)

skyBOY. *(Interjecting.)* skyBOY! "s", "k", "y", "capital B", "O", "Y" skyBOY! One word. Like Fabio.

RABBI. skyBOY! Mark, Dori.

DORI. Hi Rabbi.

RABBI. *Jerry's kids:* Gary, Todd and the empty chair is for their brother Abe, who, after graduating high school in 1978, joined the Marines and is now stationed in Amsterdam. We hope he is well.

GARY. (H) alevay.

RABBI. And Harvey's daughters Risa and her sister, Melissa.

(Very subtly, MARLENA takes her gum out of her mouth and motions to HARVEY to find something to put it in. He takes out a piece of paper and she sticks it on the paper. He wraps it up and hands it to her and she puts the wrapper in the breast pocket of his jacket.)

RABBI. *(Continues.)* She loved her grandchildren so very much that she attended every one of their graduations and even Dori's passing of her high school equivalency test!

(DORI stands up and takes a bow. VLAD eyes HELGA and points to the pillow by his feet again. She is embarrassed, but complies and comes and sits down next to him. VLAD pats her on the head, which visibly annoys her. HELEN KRANTZ is alone, so GARY asks her to sit between him and TODD.)

ELSIE. Yay Dori!

RABBI. But Sylvia was especially close to one grandchild: her grandson Gary. *(GARY motions the RABBI to stop, as he is helping HELEN into a seat next to him.)* No, Gary. This must be said, people have to know this about you. Gary was a model grandchild. He fulfilled yet another of our sacred mitzvot by caring for the sick when Sylvia broke her hip on the S.S. Carnival on the way to Paradise Island. Gary moved up here from Miami to care for his grandmother and it was in his loving arms, and his embrace that our beloved Sylvia left us.

(RABBI returns to the podium.)

GARY. Where was everybody? *(To audience member.)* You said you were coming to the hospital and you never showed up. Now you come dressed for bingo? *(Waits a beat.)* I'm sorry, I'm upset.

RABBI. But we cannot vividly remember Sylvia without mentioning her dear brother Dave, with whom she would drink and toast a few L'Chaims.

DAVE. Sometimes more than a few.

(ELSIE and DAVE giggle at this. They look like Stella Stevens and Ernest Borgnine in The Poseidon Adventure—*like a couple who went too many times to the Playboy Club.)*

RABBI. But always in celebration of the times and seasons of our calendar. And of course, Dave always picked up the tab.

DAVE. Ver Den?

(ELSIE taps DAVE's shoulder and he gets up and rejoins ELSIE on the bench.)

RABBI. We can say that our Sylvia lived a rich and long life.

HELEN KRANTZ. Not long enough Rabbi!

GARY. *(Aside —to HELEN.)* Shah still.

RABBI. And she enjoyed the less strenuous aspects of communal Jewish life with her long-standing weekly card game of 25 years, which she played with her dear friend Helen Krantz.

HELEN KRANTZ. *(Crying out.)* Oh, Sylvia darling, I miss you so much!

DORI. Shut up!

skyBOY. Dori!

RABBI. Sylvia's chair at the card table will remain empty, Dori...

skyBOY. Ha ha!

RABBI. ... and her witty repartee is silenced now and forever. Our people, her family, her friends, and all the mourners in Zion weep heavy tears at the loss of this eishes chayl, this great woman of valor. Mishaneh Makum, mishaneh mazal, our sages taught. Sylvia's place has changed now for the last time. Zichrono livracha, l'olom vaw'-ed. May her memory be to each of us for peace and a blessing now and forever. *(NATALIE reaches over to make peace with MARLENA, but MARLENA gives her the finger from behind the fan.)* Let us all say, Amen together now with one full voice.

(Everyone in unison:)

ALL. Amen.

skyBOY and DORI. Amen together now with one full voice.

(skyBOY and DORI slap each other a loud high-five. The RABBI looks at them with mild recrimination.)

skyBOY. *(To audience member.)* How come you didn't say it like that? He told you to say it like that. You're not paying attention.

RABBI. At this time we remember Sylvia as a vibrant woman who loved culture. So first, I call forward... *(MARK tells skyBOY that he is going to be called up first. So skyBOY stands up. When he hears MELISSA's name, he sits down and slaps MARK loudly.)* Sylvia's granddaughter Melissa Franklin who will play her flute* in honor of her grandmother. *(*Or whatever musical instrument the actress plays.)* Melissa, please.

(MELISSA walks timidly to the stage. She takes her instruments out of its case. BYRON rises and crosses toward the stage stopping at skyBOY's row.)

BYRON. Excuse me, Rabbi.

RABBI. Yes, Doctor Franklin.

BYRON. Before my lovely wife plays one note on her flute*, can I ask why I didn't receive a yamaha?

HELGA. *(Very embarrassed, she starts running up to him.)* I'm sorry, sweetheart. I don't know how that could've happened. *(When she reaches him.)* I just didn't see you, that's all.

(HELGA pulls a yarmulke from her pocket and places it on his head. She realizes it's white and not black like everyone else's.)

skyBOY. *(To HELGA.)* That's racist! What's the matter with you? Putting a white yarmulke on a black man! I'm calling Oprah!

(HELGA runs back to her seat. FREDO stops BYRON and trades his black yarmulke for his white one. He turns to RISA:)

FREDO. I told you I wanted a white one like the Pope.

(FREDO returns to his seat.)

BYRON. *(To RACHEL.)* I felt like a damn Q-Tip.

(BYRON returns to his seat.)

RACHEL. Welcome to the family.
MELISSA. I'm sorry. I'm just feeling a little ferklempt. Forgive me, I haven't played in a long time. It's just so hard losing Grandma...
VLAD. It's not that hard. Mother and I lost her twice today already.
MELISSA. Excuse me! *(With nostalgic rhapsody.)* When I was younger Grandma always used to say, "Melissa, *(Impersonates Grandma's concern:)* what's wrong with you? You're so shy. No one in this family is shy." Right Daddy?
HARVEY. That's right.

(MARLENA shoots him a dirty look as if to say he can't do anything right.)

MELISSA. "Always locked up in the room with your books. You should take up an instrument—the flute* Melissa. It'll bring you out a little." So than years later she said to me, "Melissa, you're still so shy and locked up in the room with that damn flute already! What are you doing with that flute?" *(Starts to jerk off her instrument unconsciously and tentatively.)* I think you're in love with the flute.

(MELISSA stops when she realizes what she has been doing.)

FREDO. *(After audience responds.)* She was getting ready for the trombone! That's what she was doing.

MELISSA. "You should take up law, Melissa, use that kepele. It'll bring you out a little. Now go get your flute and play me a song." Well, Grandma, you didn't get your concert flutist, but you sure got your lawyer. Now I want to play you a song. Excuse me while I tune up.

MARLENA. Now she has to tune? She couldn't tune before?

HARVEY. You always tune up before you play.

(MELISSA turns her back to mourners and bends over. She is wearing a fairly short skirt. Her father HARVEY tries to get her attention and tells her to stand up. The RABBI apologizes to the front rows. He asks them to turn their heads away. He places his prayer book between MELISSA's bottom and the front row. MELISSA says she's tuning her flute.)

HARVEY. *(To MELISSA.)* Melissa—
MELISSA. Daddy, give me one second to tune up!

(MELISSA crosses to other side of stage and moons the other half of the audience.)

HARVEY. Melissa, you're mooning the mourners.

(This makes MELISSA stand up straight. She waits a beat and then turns around and faces everyone.)

FREDO. *(Comment to RISA.)* She looks just like her father without the beard.

MELISSA. This was one of Grandma's favorite melodies. Feel free to hum along.

(MELISSA plays "Hatikva." ELSIE falls asleep during MELISSA's presentation.)

HELEN KRANTZ. *(She takes MELISSA's suggestion too far and sings much too loudly and off pitch.)* Hatikva! La, la, la, la, la, la (until song stops.)

(MELISSA plays until she breaks down in tears half way through the song.)

MARLENA. She didn't have to cry. She didn't play that bad.

MELISSA. You are not my mother! You have no respect for me!

MARLENA. Respect! Please! Those pantyhose are living proof that one size does *not* fit all.

(BYRON walks MELISSA back to her seat.)

RABBI. Melissa, please, before you sit dcwn I think what should be said is, "thank you, we all appreciated that gift very much."

GARY. From the heart.

RABBI. Now I'd like to call up to the bima Sylvia's... *(Again skyBOY gets up and sits down annoyed when he hears DORI's name.)* ... granddaughter Dori Grossman who will read a poem in honor of her grandmother. Dori, please.

skyBOY. *(Not too loud.)* Don't embarrass us. Use your diaphragm.

(DORI walks toward FREDO and looks for approval.)

ELSIE. Dori, honey, this way.

(DORI walks up to the stage very seductively and takes a matchbook out of her bra.)

MARLENA. You can do it honey. Just like you learned with *Hooked-on-Phonics.*

ELSIE. *(Pause.)* Take your time, girlfriend.

DORI. G-d couldn't be everywhere, so He created Grandmothers.

(MARK gives DORI a standing ovation. He only claps three times so DAVE can say his line.)

UNCLE DAVE. *(As DORI starts to leave the stage.)* Wait a minute. What kind of *fakachta* poem was that? *(Pause.)* It didn't even rhyme.

DORI. It's a Haiku. (Pronounced *hi-koo*.)

(DORI takes her seat.)

UNCLE DAVE. *(Quietly, thinking she has sneezed.)* Gesundheit.

RABBI. Next I would like to call forward Sylvia's grandson...

skyBOY *(Rising.)* Finally.

RABBI. Gary Grossman...

skyBOY. Oh, man!

RABBI. ... who will pay a loving tribute to his grandmother. Gary?

GARY. I'm sorry Rabbi but my cousin skyBOY seems anxious to go. Gey gezunterheyd, Stuart, believe me, I'm in no hurry to go up there.

skyBOY. No Gary, you Gei gezintaheh. I'll just sit my fat ass back down one more time!

(skyBOY sits down angrily.)

HELEN KRANTZ. *(Aside.)* He sings like his grandmother. (To GARY.) You'll be wonderful!

GARY. Don't give me a kinahorrah! *(As he's walking to the Bima.)* Rabbi, I don't feel good, I need something to drink. *(To audience.)* Does anybody have something to drink?

ELSIE. *(Looking in her purse.)* Do you want some Kahlua?

GARY. *(When GARY gets on stage he thanks the RABBI for a lovely service and drinks the RABBI's tea on the bima.)* I'm sorry, I'm a little phlegmy. *(He takes a slurping sip of tea.)* I should have known I was going to get sick taking care of Grandma all week long, day and night at Coney Island Hospital *(He turns around to the immediate family.)* mostly by myself...

ELSIE. What's he talking about? You were there almost every day.

GARY. ... I don't mean anything bad by that, Elsie, please. But Rabbi Wolfe said something to me on the phone last night and I'd like to share it with everyone if that's okay? Thank you. He said, "Gary a funeral, right now, is the time to speak mameloshn—" do you know what that means? Tell it like it is. tokhes oyfn tish—put your cards on the table! *(He slams his hands on the bima.)* And that's what I'm going to try to do today. Because if you can't be honest, if you can't be real with your family and friends, then who the hell can you ever be yourself with? Am I right? Thank you. I wasn't sure what I was going to say tonight, and then I unexpectedly had a little free time on my hands *when I was forced to pick my grandmother up off of the side of the Belt Parkway!* I'm in the back of a taxi cab... with Mohammed Saleem driving ... and that's when it hit me.

skyBOY. *(Aside.)* I'd like to hit him.

GARY. Her Yiddish expressions. But there is one in particular. I hope to G-d I'm not the only one who remembers her saying it, so please help me out if you recognize it: "Ales ineynem iz nishto bay keynem." *(GARY waits for audience to say "iz nisht. bay keynem" with him.)* Thank you. She lives on in some of us. All by one is by no one. And Grandma really lived her whole life for Grandpa. She really didn't come alive until Grandpa died. That sounded terrible. I don't mean that in a bad way. I really don't. But I think some of you ladies know what I'm talking about. I can't believe it Helen, is it six months already?

HELEN KRANTZ. Yes darling. Six months ago...

(HELEN KRANTZ and GARY touch hands.)

GARY. ... When Grandma broke her hip on the S.S. Carnival and nobody here had the money to pay for a home care attendant...

DAVE. Gary, I couldn't, it was during the recession—

GARY. Uncle Dave please, do you hear me blaming you? This is hard enough, give me a break. I said, I'd give up six months out of my life... *(Sadly.)* seven months ... whatever it takes until she was on her feet again. And I know I was there for her. And the very first night she was thoughtful enough to make me my favorite dinner, a little sweet and sour tongue. *(Audience moans. He reacts.)* It was good. And afterwards, with a broken hip, she propped herself up against the kitchen sink to do the dishes! I said, "Nu Grandma, what do you think I flew up from North Miami Beach for? Let me help you with the dishes." She pushed me away from the sink like an NFL linebacker. That's the martyr she was. She wouldn't take any help. *(To audience member.)* You tried to help her, I remember. Thank you. So I went into the shower and I started to sing— *(Long pause. Sometimes audience members will ask, "What did you sing?")*—"The Way We Were" the way my mother likes me to. *(MARLENA sarcastically smirks at NATALIE.)* And I just want to say thank you to those few of you who have been nice enough to ask about my mother Sandy today. G-d bless you. I promise when I am back in Florida I will convey your good wishes to her.

JERRY. Come on she's on prozac.

GARY. I wonder why she's on prozac. This coming from a man who voted for _____. *(A current right wing candidate's name.)* So that night, *(To JERRY.)* your mother said to me, "No Gavrel, sing "Romania Romania." So I sang it for her: she loved that song. And the next night, I thought I'd surprise her, so I started to givalder like a nut in the shower *(Singing.)* "Romania, Romania" and she said "No Gabriel sing "Mein Shtetl Belz," sing "Belz" to the rafters." So I sang "Belz" for her. She loved "Belz" even more. But honestly, it started getting to the point where she was making so many requests that I couldn't take a shower in peace. I was doing an entire Joel Grey concert every night in the shower. Life's funny. I never thought I'd tell this story to anybody, much less at her funeral... But Thursday night—was it Thursday night Helen?

HELEN KRANTZ. Yes darling, it was Thursday night.

GARY. Helen Krantz, gute neshome that you are, mamala, turned to me in the hospital room and she said, "Gar, Grandma's sleeping now, she won't know the difference anymore. You really need to go home and take a shower." So I did.

MARLENA. Are you going to be wrapping this up any time soon?

GARY. Can we have a little rachmoonus today of all days? One day, Uncle Harvey, you'll see, she's going to learn that the dreydl dreyt zikh! I'd like to now, PLEASE, pay tribute to a woman who never once had a bad word to say about anybody, even when she had the right to. So please Mrs. Helsenrott, now is the time to do what we rehearsed...

HELGA. I don't know, you know, Gary, we are trying out a new D.J. for that shmegegie Club Mortuary. I don't know if anyone is back there...

(VLAD questions her about what she rehearsed with GARY. HELGA tries to get the D.J.'s attention.)

GARY. *(To HELGA.)* Please! Why are you doing this to me?

(To MARLENA.) You know what, Aunt Marlena? This is the first time in all your years of name-dropping that I've ever had the opportunity to meet any of your show business friends. It couldn't hurt my career they should hear me sing a few numbers.

MARLENA. This is not a audition for you Gary. Big career! He's a singing waiter at Carolina's in Coney Island. And now I hear the restaurant is going take-out only.

GARY. *(GARY sits on the stool and pulls up his Chanukah socks.)* I just want to get comfortable. She made them at the J.C.C.

HELGA. *(Indicating for D.J. to start music.)* Okay, hit it!

GARY. Please.

HELGA. Please.

GARY. *(Sings.)*

MA MAMA MAMA MAMA MAMA MAMA MA
MA MA MA MA MA MA MA MA MA MA MA MA
MAMA MAMA MAMA MAMA MA—

MARLENA. This is not a revival of *The Jazz Singer*, Gary.

GARY.

A YIDDISHAH MAMA—MA MA MA MA MA MA MA MA
A YIDDISHKITE GRANDMA—MA MA MA MA MA MA
MA MA

MOMELE, MOMELE, MOTHER DEAR I'LL ALWAYS
    LOVE YOU MOMELE.
*WHAT'S THE USE OF TALKING, IT'S AS PLAIN AS
    PLAIN.
JUST FROM WHERE I GOT MY GOOD SENSE AND
    MY BRAIN.
ALL MY BETTER QUALITIES, MY LOOKS AND
        CHARMS FROM A CERTAIN MARRIED LADY
        THAT I LOVE TO PIECES—

*For information on performance rights to this song, see page 2.

GRANDMA.
GRANDMA GRANDMA GRANDMA GRANDMA
WHY'D YOU HAVE TO BE MADE SO PERFECTLY
          MAMANU?
GRANDMA GRANDMA GRANDMA GRANDMA
WHO COULD I EVER SEE HALF SO GOOD FOR ME
          MAMANU?
WHERE COULD I EVER MEET A GIRL AS SWEET TO
          MAKE ME CARE?
NO MATTER WHAT A HONEY, NO MATTER HOW MUCH
          MONEY, WHERE'S THE ONE TO COMPARE? TO
          MY OWN
GRANDMA GRANDMA GRANDMA GRANDMA
HOW CAN I HELP IF I PASS THE OTHER GOILIES BY,
          BY, BY
THOUGH I KEEP WIDE AWAKE AND LOOKING FOR
          A GIRL THAT I CAN TAKE HOME AND ADORE
THEY JUST DON'T SEEM TO MAKE EM ANYMORE
          LIKE MY OWN
GRANDMA GRANDMA GRANDMA GRANDMA
          GRANDMA.
*(After the second "GRANDMA" in the last line, the name
GARY!, in flashing lights, appears behind him.)*

MARLENA. What do you think they're bringing back *Star
Search*, Gary? You think Ed McMahon's here?

GARY. *(Crosses to the coffin, speaking.)* If she ever tucked
you into bed at night, you should recognize this. Please sing
along for Grandma. *(Singing.)* Goodnight, sleep tight, wake
up in the morning bright, hoodle doodle doodle. *(Speaking.)* I
love you. I love ya.

MARLENA. Pitiful! Absolutely pitiful!

skyBOY. *(As GARY walks off the stage.)* Oh great! I get to follow Liza Minnelli.

GARY. *(To person in front row.)* I'm sorry I spit on you.

RABBI. Gary, clearly it should be said: Yasher koyekh.

GARY. Thank you Rabbi. Whatever that means.

(GARY returns to his seat.)

RABBI. Now I call forward Sylvia's... *(Again skyBOY stands up.)* ... great niece.

skyBOY. *(He sits.)* Oh, forget this!

RABBI. Rachel Rosenbaum.

RACHEL. That's *Doctor* Rachel Rosenbaum.

RABBI. I'm sorry. Dr. Rachel Rosenbaum, who will share a few of her thoughts with us about her Great Aunt Sylvia.

RACHEL. Thank you very much Rabbi. *(As she is walking to the stage, she shakes the hand of an audience member.)* Former patient of mine.

ELSIE. You look very nice, honey.

RACHEL. Thank you... Elsie.

ELSIE. Jacqueline Smith Collection? K-Mart.

RACHEL. *(Pause.)* We have gathered together today to pay our respects to my Great Aunt Sylvia. Not only was she my Great Aunt, she was also my great friend. In my family, my mother always told the wonderful Aunt Sylvia stories, and it's a shame that she couldn't be with us to hear those stories, but she took ill and couldn't make the flight from West Palm Beach. In any case, when Gary called to tell me that Aunt Sylvia had passed away, I was filled with wonderful memories. Probably the healthiest childhood memories I have are centered around my Great Aunt Sylvia—

JERRY. Is this about *you?*

RACHEL. *(To JERRY.)* Excuse me. *(Pause.)* I can remember one Passover when...

JERRY. *(Muttering.)* She should see a shrinker.

RACHEL. You know I'm encountering feelings of hostility in the room!

JERRY. You should.

RACHEL. Perhaps we should confront the real issue. My book. Obviously my book *Mommy, Look at Me,* which has been on the best seller list for the past 26 weeks, has apparently raised a few issues for a few members of this family.

DAVE. Rachel, you wrote about me all through your book, and I didn't even understand one word.

RACHEL. Grandpa that's not you. That's Grandpa Rosenbaum! You're in my next book *Daddy, Give It To Me.* My cousin Gary was absolutely right. Today is the day that we should put our cards on the table. For the record, I did not write *Mommy, Look At Me* for the sole purpose of letting the world know that my family is a dysfunctional circus. However, I find it highly ironic that here we are all paying tribute to the one functional member of this family. Aunt Sylvia was the matriarch of this family. She was more of a mother to us than any of our own mothers. I'm sitting in the back of the service today noticing that none of the mothers of this family are in attendance. Where are the mothers of this family? And what have they been replaced with? *(Referring to ELSIE and NATALIE.)* Well, here are two classic examples of the Madonna-Whore complex! *(ELSIE and NATALIE get upset.)* From Grandpa to Jerry, through the generations of this family—and let's not ignore Harvey and Marlena's Wendy-Peter Pan dilemma. Where are the Madonna's, the mothers of this family?

Well, I'll tell you. They've all abandoned their children. And look at the consequences. *(She goes into the audience.)* All my cousins—skyBOY! Mark! Dori!—Three small children abandoned by their mother. She died an accidental death due to hospital negligence—

DAVE. Rachel! Ganoog ... Enough already! Vus is geven is geven. It was not my fault.

RACHEL. Grandpa, I'm speaking. You've been speaking throughout the service. Frankly, I'd think you'd be ashamed showing up at your own sister's funeral with a woman half your age.

DAVE. She's not that young.

(ELSIE gets mad at DAVE and turns away from him.)

RACHEL. We'll discuss your second childhood later. *(She walks over to where GARY and TODD are sitting.)* My poor fragile cousins—poor co-dependent Gary, sexually compulsive Todd, and their brother Abe who is not with us today. Their mother retreated from reality. She's in a mental institution, and their brother Abe pulled a geographic and followed in their mother's footsteps. And Jerry, I blame you for Abe's not being here! *(JERRY comes at RACHEL to scare her. NATALIE holds him back just in time.)* Oh, you're gonna hit me Jerry? You're gonna hit me like you hit your boys when they were growing up?

JERRY. It would probably turn you on.

RACHEL. Why don't you take a swing at Natalie too while you're at it? I'm sure we would all love to witness that.

NATALIE. Rachel, take a look at yourself!

RACHEL. Take a look at myself? You want to bring a child

into this world with that man. Take a look at your inner rage, Jerry!

JERRY. I'll show you some inner rage!

(NATALIE pulls him back to his seat. MELISSA goes to comfort RACHEL.)

RACHEL. I'm fine, Melissa. My cousins Melissa and Risa—now their mother Rena was a smart woman. She escaped this family all together. She took off to Paris with her gynecologist.

RISA. That's not true! It was her podiatrist.

RACHEL. And my mother. Let's not forget my mother. My mother's not sick in West Palm Beach. My mother hasn't had a sick day in her life. She's been in seclusion ever since my book was published! The only reason I'm here today is to see the woman in the casket. My Great Aunt Sylvia, the sole female support of this family. *(Out of control.)* Frankly, Aunt Sylvia, you don't know how lucky you are not to be alive today to see how incredibly dysfunctional and in denial your family has become! *(Suddenly devoid of emotion.)* Thank you very much.

(RACHEL sits down. Aside to audience member: "I don't usually act out.")

MELISSA. *(Softly as the RABBI says his line.)* You have some ego! This is not one of your seminars!

RABBI. And finally, after a few false starts, I call forward Sylvia's grandson Stuart Grossman.

MELISSA. *(Aside to GARY.)* Don't let him go up there.

GARY. *(Aside to MELISSA.)* I'm not a censor.

skyBOY. skyBoy!

RABBI. I'm sorry, skyBoy Grossman. Who has created a piece of performance art to honor the memory of his grandmother. skyBoy, now please.

skyBOY. The moment has passed, Rabbi. Move on.

(MARLENA urges everybody to coax him to go up.)

GARY. Keep going, Rabbi!

DORI. *(She hits skyBOY.)* Stuart, get up there!

(DORI starts applauding and tries to work the audience into a frenzy chanting, skyBOY! skyBOY!)

skyBOY. *(To GARY.)* Now you're going to see some real talent, Gary.

GARY. I doubt it!

skyBOY. *(As he walks to stage.)* Someone should tell him that vaudeville's dead! *(To RABBI.)* Yo Rabbi. *(Softly.)* Can you move the podium to the center?

(skyBOY goes over to MARLENA and takes her direction.)

RACHEL. Excuse me—I'm sorry skyBOY, I'd like to apologize.

RISA and MELISSA. Good!

RACHEL. For forgetting to mention I'll be doing a book signing at the Barnes and Noble at 82nd and Broadway.*(**Or an equivalent local bookstore.)* My colleagues Marianne Williamson and Christina Crawford will be in attendance. I hope you can all join us. Thank you. *(Aside.)* After Shiva.

(RACHEL sits down.)

skyBOY. Rachel, I feel your pain. NOW LET IT GO!!

RACHEL. Thank you, skyBoy.

RABBI. The following performance has been made possible by funding by the Marlena Weiss-Grossman Foundation.

HARVEY. What!?

MARLENA. *(To HARVEY.)* I send half your disability check each month to my nephew. Now shah.

HARVEY. Why?

MARLENA. I'm doubling your medication when we get home.

(skyBOY whispers more directions to the RABBI. The RABBI reluctantly spins the propeller on the beanie that skyBOY is wearing. The music begins. MARLENA coaches skyBOY through his performance. skyBOY takes out a can of candied yams. He does a modern dance to the opening bars of Richard Strauss's Also Sprach Zarathustra.)

skyBOY. *(Song ends.)*

Part Two.

(Should daven prior to saying:)

Vy Vy Vy Vy Vy did you die? (2x.)

Ashes to ashes
dust to dust
you loved me
you smothered me
with your 40 double D bust.

Vy Vy Vy Vy Vy did you die? (2x.)

Gran Gran Gran Grand Union - Wednesday is double-cou-
pon day
Gran Gran Gran Grandfather clock - tic toc tic toc
Gran Gran Gran Grand Prix - Vroooom
(To audience.) I'm trying to say something, stay with me.
Okay.

Sylvia ... Sylvia
via NY
via Miami
via Jerusalem
maybe next year
(As SYLVIA.)
Stuart darling
Don't be a loser like Gary
be a doctor
eat your fruit Stuart
That's abuse Grandma
my mother said I didn't have to
my mother wouldn't have made me
you're not my mother
my mother's dead
and now so are you
and now it's my turn
Grandma ... be a doctor
Grandma ... eat your fruit
(Tongue tied.) Grandma ... eat a doctor
Be a fruit!
take a look at my *(Drops his pants.)*

fruit of the looms *(Moons grandma.)*

(Sings.) Moon over Miami, moon over Miami...

(HARVEY, and RABBI rush skyBOY. skyBOY runs off stage screaming. MARK follows him out.)

Leave me alone. I'm not finished yet. Gary got to finish his song. This is censorship. You can't sell flowers in a fish market. *(To audience.)* What are you looking at?

(skyBOY exits.)

GARY. *(Comment.)* You should have stopped after the first part. Blasphemous!

RACHEL. *(Comment.)* He had too much sugar this morning.

HARVEY. *(Aside to MARLENA.)* Of all the charities in the world you give money to skyBOY.

MARLENA. *(Comment to HARVEY while applauding skyBOY and crying.)* You just don't get it, Harvey. You're not hip.

HARVEY. *(Aside.)* Thank G-d I'm not hip.

RABBI. Well, that concludes the *cultural* aspect of our service. *(Reading.)* Now since Mrs. Grossman's internment will be in Brooklyn so she can rust with her husband Harry...

ELSIE. Rust?

RABBI. Rest. Rest. I'm sorry. Rest with her husband Harry. The graveside ceremony with El Molei Rachamin and Kaddish will be conducted there at Washington Cemetery in Brooklyn. For those of you who would like to offer your love and consolation to the family, after the completion of the internment at the cemetery, shiva will be held at Mrs. Grossman's home.

MARLENA. Oh, no Rabbi, excuse me. I'm having a surprise shiva at Planet Hollywood.* *(*Or flashy, popular local club.)* And something fabulous is coming from Zabar's.* *(*Or name of costly local caterer.)* You're going to love it!

GARY. *(Aside to MELISSA and RISA.)* Did you know about this?

MELISSA. *(To GARY.)* She has mad cow disease.

RISA. *(To GARY.)* Tell her!

RABBI. Gary? Was I supposed to know about this?

GARY. Rabbi, she's obviously crossed over. Please say something to her.

RABBI. Marlena, there is no such thing as a surprise shiva.

MARLENA. Rabbi, you don't understand...

RABBI. Marlena, please.

MARLENA. ... All of my mother-in-law's favorite couples are going to be there.

RABBI. It is customary for shiva to be held at the home of the deceased. And that is where it must be held. I'm sorry.

MARLENA. Boring.

RABBI. The meal of consolation...

HELEN KRANTZ. Excuse me Rabbi, don't you mean the Mitzvah meal?

RABBI. Thank you for helping *again*, Helen. The Mitzvah meal will be held in a few moments downstairs in the Helsenrott Bistro.

HELGA. *(Aside.)* Vestibule.

RABBI. And I understand that Natalie Chasen, Jerry's...

MARLENA. Tramp.

RABBI. ... significant other, who by the way is in the process of conversion—

DAVE.	HELEN KRANTZ.
(To NATALIE.) Mazel Tov.	Mazel Tov.

(HARVEY reaches over to shake her hand and MARLENA cuts him a look which causes him to back away.)

RABBI. ... she has selected the menu for the meal.

NATALIE. Yes, it's going to be a five-course fleshy dick meal—

GARY. *(Aside.)* It's a hard word to wrap your tongue around.

HARVEY. *(He interrupts her and tries to teach her the correct pronunciation of the world.)* Natalie, that's fleisha dic. Long A.

NATALIE. Flasha dick meal blessed by my teacher Rabbi Postrel, and it's in celebration of the fruits of Paradise.

(NATALIE motions to her breasts as if they're part of the offering.)

RABBI. *(To NATALIE.)* That's nice. The uh...

NATALIE. Pineapples.

RABBI. So, in a moment we will be exiting the Helsenrott Chapel through the Helsenrott Foyer going down to the Helsenrott Bistro for the Mitzvah meal.

HARVEY Excuse me Rabbi, isn't it the meal of condolence?

RABBI. *(A bit perturbed already.)* Okay. The meal of condolence in the bistro. Thank you.

(HELEN shakes her head and makes the tsk-tsk-tsk sound of disapproval.)

HARVEY. Thank you.

VLAD. *(Flirting.)* Thank you, Rabbi Michael. Perhaps later

we can see you in your Bar Mitzvah pants. *(RABBI nervously adjusts his pants.)* Right after the meal we will all be leaving for internment services at Washington Cemetery.

HELGA. No, no. I'm sorry, sweetheart. We have to come back up here to tie up some loose ends.

VLAD. No, Mother, I don't want these people to stay. I have go-go boys coming to audition. They're going to be naked.

HELGA. Why are you doing this to me?

VLAD. *(Slowly, with a sing-song, to torture her.)* Naked... naked ... naked.

HELGA. I'm sorry he is such a kidder. Thank you, Michael, that was a beautiful service.

(VLAD takes the RABBI offstage and pinches him on the butt. DAVE quietly criticizes VLAD.)

VLAD. *(Aside to DAVE.)* Mind you own business, old man.

(HELGA turns around after witnessing VLAD pinching the RABBI's tush. She is embarrassed.)

HELGA. In a few seconds we will be going downstairs for a little nosh.

ELSIE. All right, let's eat.

HELGA. *(To ELSIE.)* No, you sit here! *(HELGA slams her pocketbook down on the bima for effect.)* I have to talk to the nice people. In a moment I am going to be sending you downstairs to eat. Now, pay attention. I'm going to be sending you down row by row. I'll start at the back of the chapel first and work my way to the front. Please do not get up, do not get into the aisles. Even if you have to make a pish. There is a reason for this. I've got big tsuris with the fire department. I just got a four hundred dollar summons. Too many people up, too many people in the aisle. You wait for me, I'll tell you when to go. Now when I get to you I'll point to your row, you stand up and exit one behind the other, just like Hebrew School. *(Pause.)* Now when you go downstairs you will see two tables with food. *(At the end of her rope, with great hysteria.) On each table is the same food!* So you go downstairs and make yourself up a plate and come right back here to the chapel, take your seat, put your plate in your lap and you eat, like a pic-nik. Because I understand some family members have some very important announcements they'd like to share with everyone. So after you go downstairs, make yourself a nice plate, take your food, exit out the long hallway where you first entered, go outside and you make a little u-e-turn. And at this time, those of you who must shmoke, like Uncle David, please do that outside, don't stink up my "holeway."

ELSIE. He don't light it.

HELGA. The rest of you come back inside and we can continue with the funeral services. And now we will all go down for a little nosh of bagels and cream cheese.

NATALIE. No no Helga, there must be some mistake. I ordered Chollupshus, chicken soup with knadelox...

JERRY. *(Corrects her.)* Knadeloch.

NATALIE. ... knadeloch, platters of pachaz, and was it six gallons? *(JERRY shakes his head no and whispers in her ear.)* Seven gallons of griebenes!

HELGA. I'm sorry, sweetheart. All I saw downstairs was some bagels and cream cheese. Please go downstairs and speak to my son Vlad and straighten it out.

NATALIE. *(As she exits.)* _____*(Audience member's name. In the front of the house.)* brought a shank bone sculpture from _____ *(Local butcher's shop.)* Mark, Dori, my niece and nephew will you kids get the fruit baskets and *(As she's bounding through the back of the house.)* _____ *(Audience member's name.)* made a noodle kugel with the Sunmaid raisins.

HELGA. Please, immediate family only, make your exodus to the food now...

(An anthem, like the theme from Exodus, *plays as the family exits down the aisle.)*

THE MITZVAH MEAL

*(HELGA starts with the last two rows of the house and sends
them downstairs like a commandant. (Ex. "Don't anybody
get up behind me or I'll trip over you as I'm backing up.
Wait for me!") She works her way to the front of the house.
The RABBI mingles with all the mourners. GARY asks the
RABBI to call I.J. Morris to get a hearse for the end of the
funeral. He also asks the RABBI to stay until the end of the
funeral, even though he only paid him for the eulogy.
After the immediate family goes downstairs:
HELEN follows UNCLE DAVE because she has been in love
with him ever since they had an affair right after WWII. He
tells her "not now," but she follows him anyway.*

*FREDO goes up to the stage. He takes out his rosary beads
and proceeeds to kneel down as if he were praying to
SYLVIA. RISA sees this and is horrified. She runs to the
stage and tries to get FREDO off of his knees. She asks the
front row, "Did you tell him to do this?" RISA finally asks
BYRON to help. He eventually succeeds getting FREDO
off the floor. RISA is upset, and MELISSA consoles her
enroute to the meal.*

*NATALIE, DORI, and MARK are the first to arrive downstairs
where the food is displayed. MARK gets a plate made and
makes his way back upstairs to the chapel, where he tells
people that he is going to feed Grandma.*

*VLAD comes down and he has a fight with NATALIE. She
asks him where the food is:)*

NATALIE. Where's my meat? Why can't I find my meat?

(VLAD tells NATALIE that the American Express card number that she gave him was bad. GARY joins the fight later on and tells VLAD how he is going to get his cousin MELISSA to sue him.)

GARY. Shmuckuhluvitch, get over here!

VLAD. The name is Helsenrott!

GARY. That name is yutz! My stepmother is known in Miami for her spread—

VLAD. I bet she is!

GARY. This is not the food she ordered. Bring it out or you're going to have a lawsuit! My cousin Melissa studied with Leslie Abramson and I have all of the original receipts! You have two minutes to put your meat on this table.

(GARY asks men to tell the distraught NATALIE that they like her spread.

skyBOY is outside asking people if they understood and liked his performance art piece. He shmoozes and mingles with the mourners throughout the mitzvah meal. He suddenly gets upset about his mother dying when he was a boy.

MARLENA tries to get Sly or Demi on the phone to no avail. When people ask her about her water bottle she replies, "A woman can never be too lubricated." She hocks HARVEY to go to the food table three times before he makes her a plate that she is satisfied with. She finds HELEN KRANTZ a "shtupping partner" for a soft porn movie for the elderly set that she is going to start working on. MARLENA promises auditions for all the mothers/

daughters in the audience for the Massengil Douche com-
mercial she'll be working on.
NATALIE sees MARLENA eating fruits and vegetables.)

NATALIE. Well, isn't this nice. You complained about the
food but you're eating it.

MARLENA. I'm not eating the food. Just the vegetables.

NATALIE. Well, that's good. It'll help to clean out some
of the toxins in your body.

MARLENA. I don't have any toxins in my body. My co-
lon is so clean you can eat off of it.

NATALIE. That's just what I want to do. Eat off your co-
lon.

MARLENA. Not literally. Figuratively.

(TODD starts flirting with AVA who is wearing two strands of
beads. GARY reminds him that she looks just like their
mother.)

GARY. Nice set of beads. Gerard? Is that a Jewish name?

AVA. I changed it. The name Jerry has special significance
to me.

GARY. Oh, but you're Jewish?

AVA. Yes.

GARY. You look like my mother. Helen Krantz thought
you were her when you walked in. That's a compliment. She's
the prettiest out of all three daughters-in-law. And a real
balabusta. Still is. *(Whispers to TODD.)* Leave her alone, she
looks just like mommy.

(HELEN KRANTZ is downstairs putting bagels in plastic

baggies telling the onlookers that it is for the poor.
TODD flirts with the other women and entices some to smoke
pot with him in the Bistro.
HELEN KRANTZ tells AVA that she's glad that she came and
that the hormones have done wonders for her. AVA asks
HELEN not to tell anyone and HELEN promises.
HELEN scolds RACHEL for telling the mourners about fam-
ily secrets. But also tells her she looks wonderful and that
she enjoyed reading her book. HELEN also tells RACHEL
that MELISSA is pregnant.
MELISSA tells DORI to stay away from FREDO and that RISA
is going through some rough times. DORI guesses that RISA
is still bulimic. DORI immediately goes to RISA and starts
antagonizing her about her bulimia. RISA gets upset and
runs into the bathroom and starts throwing up the food that
she just ate. MELISSA runs in after her, as does RACHEL.
They try to assure RISA that she is not fat. In the meantime
FREDO is pounding on the door demanding to know if his
wife is all right.)

FREDO. Risa come out here now! I thought bulimia was a country!

(RACHEL goes on with her psychobabble about RISA's prob-
lems.)

RACHEL. My second cousin is a sexual anorexic. She starves herself of sex and food. She's very skin-hungry too.

(RACHEL tells FREDO she knows of a good therapist in Con-
necticut for them. RACHEL then catches up with MELISSA

and tells her that she should not have a baby so soon after getting married. RACHEL also quietly tells anyone who will listen that she can't eat bagels. "Childhood trauma— the holes."
MELISSA tells her father that she's pregnant.
NATALIE plays hostess of the Mitzvah meal.)

NATALIE. We got milky dick instead of fleshy dick. But it all works out because you can eat the fleshy back at the house after eating the milky here.

(JERRY and GARY are on the sofa downstairs in the bistro mingling with all the mourners. JERRY asks where TODD is and NATALIE runs to find him. She sees him smoking pot on the other side of the room and tells him to stop before his father catches him. JERRY and GARY walks over to TODD. JERRY spots TODD smoking pot. He calmly walks up to TODD and throws TODD against the wall. NATALIE gets in between TODD and JERRY and stops the fight. GARY yells for his father to go to the coffin room. JERRY exits. GARY berates TODD for what he did and tells him to go home.)

GARY. That's great Todd! First pot and then crack! It leads to other things.

NATALIE. Jerry come back! Todd was upset. Dori gave him the drugs.

GARY. You're enabling him, Natalie. That's what my mother used to do. She made excuses for all of the men in the family.

(GARY follows JERRY to the "coffin room."

*MARLENA tells people that she gained weight by acciden-
tally counting latkes as a vegetable on her Weight Watchers program. She makes her way outside to compliment
skyBOY on his performance art piece.*

*After DORI causes trouble for RISA, FREDO gets angry with
her. DORI flirts with the RABBI. As the room empties, she
goes outside and finds ELSIE. They joke about TODD being busted. DORI tells ELSIE that she has some coke. They
flirt with men and then go inside.*

*HELEN finds DAVE at the coffin, mourning. She takes the
opportunity to remind him what a happy relationship they
had in their youth, and that Sylvia wanted them to be together. He tries to silence her. She continues that she doesn't
think it's right that he is going with a young shicker shiksa.
He defends ELSIE and shushes her. She asks him to come
and visit her because she will be lonely now that SYLVIA is
gone. As they are leaving the coffin she tells him that she
knows about ABE and that Sylvia told her she paid for it.
He shushes her about that as well.*

Everyone returns to the chapel again to take their seats.

NATALIE is making sure people smell her love oils.)

NATALIE. It's the Ode de Ova. You use only a drop in the
bathtub because it's very strong.

*(MARLENA tells people about how she got BYRON to reen-
act the O.J. murder when he visited her with MELISSA in
L.A. and then they drove in a Ford Bronco to Mezzaluna
for lunch. She thinks she can get him an audition to play
A.C. Cowlings in the miniseries, but he's not interested.*

FREDO tells people his mother sent a lasagne to the home for shiva. He's upset that the flowers he sent to the chapel aren't displayed.

When people tell MELISSA that she looks pale [The actress should put white make-up on her lips.], BYRON tells people that it's just her contrast with him.

UNCLE DAVE, AVA, and skyBOY take seats on the stage.

DORI blows a rape whistle hanging around her neck, saying, "C'mon, some of us got plans."

HELGA shushes everyone down.)

END OF ACT II

ACT III

HELGA. Can I have your attention please? You remember Marky Grossman. Marky would like to make a little speech. He's been practicing all day. I need you to quiet down because he's a little nervous. Go ahead, sweetheart.

MARK. Good evening, family and friends.

VLAD. Boo!

(MARK gets frightened. HELGA scolds VLAD.)

HELGA. Leave him alone! Okay, sweetheart. Start again.

MARK. Good evening, family and friends...

ELSIE. Marky, honey, this is not a very good evening. Think about it.

(HELGA whispers something in MARK's ear.)

MARK, Sad evening family and friends. This concludes the meal portion of our funeral service today [tonight]. We do ask at this time that you throw all garbage neatly beneath the seat in front of you. Place all cups in an upright and locked position. Thank you.

(MARK takes his hands out of his jacket pockets so that it opens up and the audience can see his open zipper with the shirt tail sticking out of it.)

MARLENA. Marky honey, your little pony is coming out of the stable.

(MARK looks at his zipper and is horrified. HELGA and VLAD try to fix his zipper.)

MARK. Vlad Helsenrott and his mom Mrs. Helsenrott have requested that I make the following announcement. There are eighteen *(He gets confused. HELGA spits the word "Chai" in his ear and we should get the sense that she has terrible breath. VLAD hands her some breath drops. MARK wipes the spit off his ear.)* Chai locations of the Helsenrott Mortuaries in the tri-state area. Please feel free to visit any one of them when the need arises. *(HELGA whispers in his ear again.)* Thank you.

(MARK leaves the stage.)

DAVE. Helga, a commercial?
HELGA. What better place?
DAVE. Not when I'm paying for it.
HELGA. *(To UNCLE DAVE.)* A few less shekels in your pocket, you'll never notice it. *(To audience.)* Now we are going to celebrate Sylvia's life the way she wanted us to and the way she lived it. Like my good friend Helen Krantz always says—
HELEN KRANTZ. Like Sholem Alechem!

HELGA. Like Sholem Alechem. But first, again a reminder, please put your plates carefully under your seats and try not to shpill the drinks. It makes sticky on the floor...

HARVEY. Excuse me, Helga. It's against Jewish law to eat with the dead. Why are we eating with the dead?

MARLENA. Big deal. I sleep with the dead!

(HARVEY moves away from MARLENA. skyBOY and VLAD do an elaborate snap.)

HELGA. I'm sorry, Harvey. We did this when Harry died, I'm sure Sylvia wouldn't mind. Now when Grandma was in the hospital she was told that she was going to have her first great grandchild by Melissa and Byron. It was Grandma's fondest wish that she would live long enough to see this first great grandchild, but it was "Nisht Bashert." On a happier note, she often told me how much she enjoyed dancing with you, Byron, at your wedding to Melissa, and she also reminded me that life does go on and that there is no greater joy in this world than welcoming a new baby into a family.

ELSIE. Here, here! I'll drink to that!

DAVE. Elsie, you've had enough already. Be careful, *(With concern.)* you're the designated driver.

HELGA. So, Melissa and Byron, in memory of your grandmother, and at her request, please won't you both come up and honor her with a dance?

(As MELISSA and BYRON approach, HELGA says Mazel Tov, congratulations, etc.)

MELISSA. How did you know?

HELGA. Oh a little birdie told me. *(Hugs BYRON a little too sexually.)* Congratulations, Dr. Franklin.

BYRON. Oh? So you can see me now?

HELGA. Of course I see you, you funny man!

BYRON. I have just a brief announcement I would like to make. Grandma always used to speak to me in Yiddish, sometimes forgetting that I wasn't Jewish. I would just nod my head as if I understood, and eventually I was able to pick up some of it. I remember at our wedding she told the Kosher Ethiopian caterer, 'der mentsh trakht un got lakht." Which means people plan and G-d laughs. Well, Grandma had always wanted a doctor in the family, and she got one. I just came in a different package, that's all. Grandma, this dance is for you.

MELISSA. Oh, by the way, if the baby's a boy we're naming him Sylvio, and if it's a girl we're going to name her Sylvia Shaniqua.

ELSIE and DORI. Shaniqua Grossman! Yo! Yo! Shaniqua in the house!

(Music starts and they dance. MELISSA gets lost in the moment and starts to hump BYRON's leg. BYRON stops her when he realizes what she is doing.)

MARK. *(Aside.)* That's the way my dogs dance!

FREDO and RISA. *(Angrily to D.J.)* Will you shut that music off please!

HELGA. I think that's enough dancing. Turn that music off. Hey! Turn it off!

(HELGA exits. RISA and FREDO approach the stage complaining that they're watching a "sex dance." The music

stops. There is a moment of tense silence.)

FREDO. Shalom.We have a little announcement that we would like to make, too. If that's okay.

MELISSA. Of course that's okay.

RISA. I guess we were the last ones to find out...

MELISSA. Come over here and wish your sister a Mazel Tov!

RISA. *(Interrupting MELISSA and speaking in an over-zealous and very forced manner.)* I'm happy for you.

(RISA hugs, kisses, and congratulates MELISSA and BYRON.)

DORI and ELSIE. *(Doing cocaine at their seats with TODD.)* NOT!

(FREDO and BYRON react to DORI and ELSIE with grimaces.)

VLAD. This is a lovely "Precious Moment Figurine," but can we get on with it?

FREDO. *(To VLAD.)* Excuse me but aren't you supposed to be asleep until midnight?

(VLAD stares furiously at FREDO and sits down. When FREDO asks for a stool for his wife, VLAD hands it to him angrily. RISA sits on the stool with her legs slightly ajar. She hands FREDO her purse.)

ELSIE. Cross your legs honey.

MARLENA. Yeah. I can practically see what she had for breakfast.

RISA. I wanted for us to come up here and be a part of this funeral—especially after so many of Grandma's friends have told me today they don't even know who I am. They keep asking me what my relation is to her. We're feeling very left out. I don't know if it's because my husband's not Jewish or because I didn't come to the hospital. Fredo and I received a few phone calls at our home in Connecticut this week that I didn't return, and it's not because I don't care. It's because I have a serious problem with hospitals. Ask my husband, I can't stand the smell of them. *(She looks at FREDO.)* Tell them.

FREDO. She can't stand the smell of hospitals.

RISA. But I did speak to Grandma once last week, and she yelled at me for the first time in my life. I though it was her medication, but I know now she wanted to see me one last time before she died. Melissa, you know, Fredo and I paved the way for you and Byron. When we first got engaged, Grandma clipped out an article about how more Jewish families were being wiped out by inter-marriage than were wiped out by World War II. I thought she had come around though, when she came to visit us one Hanukkah after we were married at our home in Brentwood, but that's when... *(FREDO whispers in her ear "don't bring that up right now")* ... in the middle of the night Grandma woke up broygez and set fire to our Christmas tree.

FREDO. She denied any responsibility. She claimed that the burning bush had returned.

RISA. I know she did these things because she was trying to save me and I forgive her, and I'm sure she forgives me for whatever I did ... so I wanted to say in front of everyone, I'm sorry I didn't go to the hospital, but Grandma knows I loved her and that's what's important. Right?

FREDO. *(He interrupts.)* I have a little surprise presentation to make...

AVA. I love surprises.

RISA. So do I. I'll tell them Fredo, this is my family, I want to make the announcement—

FREDO. *(Quietly.)* I am going to make the presentation.

(FREDO squeezes RISA's neck.)

RISA. He's such a bovan!

FREDO. Here. *(He hands RISA's purse back to her.)* My family—the Iannuzzi family—owners and operators of Iannuzzi surplus Marble Imports Incorporated, a registered trademark, would like to offer their condolences to the Grossman family—

DAVE. *(Even though he's a Schildiner, he accepts.)* Thank you.

FREDO. *(Acknowledges DAVE with a gesture.)* — by donating an eighteen foot marble statue of Our Lady of Mount Carmel to St. Lucy's Parish. It's going to be erected on the front lawn of the church with the engraving "In loving memory of Sylvia Schildiner Grossman." And we hope you can all attend the Iannuzzi Erection Ceremony.

(RISA and FREDO return to their seats.)

NATALIE. I also have something I would like to share.

MARLENA. Yeah, I bet you do!

NATALIE. *(She floats up to the stage.)* Jerry and I and the boys Gary and Todd ... and of course Abe, wherever he is, are very blessed ... so much love. And we would like to circulate some of that love energy in the form of money with a check in Sylvia's name to some of her favorite charities: the Hadassah Girls! Remember Dori how Grandma was always trying to slep you off...

DORI. Schlep.

NATALIE. ... schlep you off to the practices? Well, I guess it was another missed bashert. Well, Dori, it's not too late because tonight [today] we have some of the biggest mokers...

DAVE. *Machers*, honey.

NATALIE. *(With difficulty.)* Macher's. We have some of the biggest Machers sharing in our grief tonight [today]. The president of Hadassah International <u>audience member #1</u> *(Should find a Catholic lady.)* is here mourning with us. <u>Audience member #1</u> please stand up and take a bow. <u>Audience member #1</u> is the first Roman Catholic president to ever head up a Hadassah group. They do a wonderful job. Also my love oils company, "L'Essence"—that's French for essence—you might recognize us from the infomercial. If you stay up late enough on Saturday night, we're on right after Hair in a Can. But most of our success is due to our wonderful hair and makeup artist, <u>audience member #2</u>, please stand up. This woman/man is a Jewish saint. A lot of people don't know that <u>audience member #2</u> is the costumer for Erik Estrada, but he/she not only did Erik Estrada—

skyBOY. Who hasn't?

NATALIE. But she/he also gave Sally Struthers a whole new look. She/he's using it for SAVE THE CHILDREN!

skyBOY. I think Sally's eating those children now.

NATALIE. Our 800 number has been ringing off the hook. So we're creating a brand new love oil that's going to be ed-

ible, digestible, and full of protein and we're going to call it—
    DORI. Sperm.
    NATALIE. "L'Esprit de Sylvie" in keeping with the French
motif. And 10% of proceeds from sales will go to Sylvia's
most recent charity, the Skylake Fertility Clinic in North Miami Beach, where Jerry and I are trying to have our daughter.
Thank you.

(NATALIE bows.)

    MARLENA. Why bother? Your eggs are poached!
    NATALIE. Marlena, isn't it time for the women in this fam-
ily to support each other? To be shvesters?
    MARLENA. *(She gets up.)* First of all, *shvester,* you're not
in this family! And second of all, if you wanted support, you
should have worn a bra!
    NATALIE. All day/night long I've tried to see the goddess
in you! *(She gets off the stage and walks past MARLENA.)*
You just want my Jerry, that's all.
    MARLENA. Want him? I already had him!

(MARLENA pushes NATALIE on purpose.)

    NATALIE. Stay out of my auric field.
    MARLENA. I've had it with your airy, fairy bull—

*(MARLENA attacks and NATALIE accidentally rips
MARLENA's top down. Seeing what she's done she gets
upset and runs to JERRY.)*

    NATALIE. *(As she's running back to JERRY.)* Not my hair!

I draw the line at my hair! Now my karma is all screwed up.

(MARLENA turns and stoically walks to the stage not knowing her chest is exposed. She turns to the audience and looks at their reaction. The RABBI runs up and tells her to look at her toes. She looks down and realizes her top is down. She turns her back to the audience and pulls her top up. She turns around to the audience again. She looks at NATALIE.)

MARLENA. You will pay for humiliating me at my mother-in-law's funeral! At least mine are real.

NATALIE. *(Runs half-way down the aisle and points at her breasts.)* These are from ginseng!

MARLENA. Yeah, ginseng, and I'm really a size three. I'm just retaining water.

MELISSA. *(Aside.)* Yeah, the Hudson River.

MARLENA. Harvey and I *(She snaps her fingers for HARVEY to come to her side.)* have something we would also like to share.

(HARVEY runs to MARLENA. As he is running up, his two daughters whine.)

MELISSA and RISA. Daddy!

MARLENA. Harvey and I *(HE tries to cover her breasts to no avail. MARLENA stops him.)* are taking up a collection, so take out your wallets and checkbooks and don't be shy, for a tree of life at the Westside Jewish Community Center in Los Angeles, where Harvey spends every waking moment day and night. And I volunteer once a year. Well, I'm busy. So you can give me cash or a check today, or if you prefer, call me when

I get back to L.A. I've got to zip right back. I just got retained to do...* (*Example— The new Fox Movie of the Week, "Father of the Bride" starring Woody Allen. *Topical.) So you can call me at 1-900-MARLENA.

NATALIE. (Aside.) That's because I have an 800 number. She's so competitive.

ELSIE. You have to pay for that!

MARLENA. I know it's $12.95 a minute, but I throw in make-up tips.

ELSIE. (Aside to an audience member.) Like I need make-up tips.

(ELSIE laughs loudly.)

MARLENA. So you call, make a pledge, get a tip. Now where's Uncle Dave?

DAVE. Over here.

MARLENA. Uncle Dave, why don't you kick off this campaign for your sister by giving me a check here and now for $500,000.* (*Or any amount actress chooses to throw out.)

DAVE. Molly—

MARLENA. Yes, Uncle Dave?

DAVE. Why don't you and your groyse moyl go to hell?

MARLENA. What do you mean? You're always talking about all the money you give to everyone!

(NATALIE returns to her seat with JERRY wondering if the graceuh moyel cut the little boy's pee pee. RACHEL comes up to comfort DAVE.)

RACHEL. (An aside to DAVE.) Grandpa, did you take your

pills?

MARLENA. *(She walks half way up the aisle before she realizes that HARVEY is not with her. She barks out another order.)* Harvey! Harv? Come here.

HARVEY. No!

(HARVEY stays on stage. VLAD and skyBOY begin petting.)

MARLENA. *(To her friends she is sitting with)* A temporary testosterone rush I assure you, from a talking Chia Pet. He'll pay for that in a big way. He'll be sleeping in the hotel garage tonight.

(MARK runs on stage after GARY tells him to go make peace.)

MARK. Excuse me, please. On behalf of my very beautiful sister Dori...

ELSIE. Don't worry, Dori, everyone knows who you are.

MARK. ... and my very interesting brother skyBOY and my two yellow Labs Cupcake and Twinkies, I want to let you all know that I'll be taking care of Grandma Sylvia's grave in Brooklyn like I've been doing for Grandpa Harry all these years. So don't worry about it, I got her covered.

GARY. Very good, Mark. The grave looks beautiful. Stop sweeping off the stones.

VLAD. Okay, if that's everything, why don't we rush this little hoo-ha down to Washington Cemetery?

GARY. Excuse me. Rabbi, I think somebody should get up there and say some positive words of closure if the funeral director is going to futz around up there and say things like hoo-ha.

VLAD. What's wrong with hoo-ha?

GARY. It's like a safe sex video up there.

RABBI. Gary, I'll say something officially in a moment. But if you would like to speak, why don't you stand up in front where everybody can see you.

HELEN KRANTZ. *(As an aside.)* You tell them, Gary.

NATALIE. *(As an aside.)* It's your gift, honey. He's a shaman and a showman.

(GARY walks up to the stage.)

MARLENA. See him!? Ray Charles can see him in that suit! *(GARY looks to UNCLE HARVEY for support.)* He looks like a Jewish smurf!

GARY. It's exactly that type of negativity that I'd like to address right now. I finally got up a little appetite and I went downstairs for a little whitefish salad and there were a few people down there with such farbisn punims, you saw those matzoh faces? I went behind them to hear what they were kvetching about, and they were saying, "I don't know why we're laughing and dancing and singing at Sylvia's funeral." And I wanted to say that if you'd shown up at the hospital this week, you would have heard Grandma say to me, "Gary, please, when I'm gone don't shray and throw yourself on the ground. I don't want that kind of funeral. Celebrate my life. I lived my golden years. And when I'm gone, just give me a funeral like my girlfriend had. Remember Ida Kaplan from Starrett City? We sang show tunes as she was lowered into the grave. *Aunt Tsippy (This can be an audience member's name.)* in the back sang "Everything's Coming Up Roses." Grandma entrusted me to disseminate some of the material things she's left behind to those of us who've come to pay tribute to her today. And I had something very special, Uncle Dave, that I was going to divvy

up between Abe and Risa, but I just checked the answering
machine to see if we got a call, *(Sadly.)* no messages, so Risa
you can have them both, if you remember what I'm talking
about. Remember what Grandma used to measure you and
Abe up against in the foyer? *(He crosses to RISA and FREDO.)*
Tell me—

RISA. The Chagall windows!

GARY. The Chagall windows! Enjoy in good health both
of you. Hope you like them Frey.

FREDO. Yeah, they sound like a lot of fun.

RISA. Thank you. Can I have them delivered?

GARY. *(To HELEN KRANTZ.)* Helen, people are hocking
me in china, today out of all days. "Gary, if I should pay a
shiva call this week, is Helen Krantz going to make her vegetable kishka?"

HELEN KRANTZ. Mid far genign. With pleasure, Gary.

GARY. But with no oil.

HELEN KRANTZ. No oil?

GARY. Last time, it went right through me. Try the Egg
Beaters, you'll see. *(Cross to MELISSA.)* If I gave the impres-
sions that I was the only one at the hospital this week, I'm
sorry. I'm a little farmisht in kop. It's understandable I'd get a
little fartumlt today. So I just want to set the record straight
right now by telling everyone that your husband Dr. Franklin,
Byron, was in Grandma's hospital room every morning this
week, 6:30 a.m. opening the blinds in Grandma's room so the
sun would shine in on her face when she woke up, and he sang
"The Candy Man" to her every single morning. And Byron,
this is true, he always thinks I'm kibbutzing with him but Helen
Krantz was there when it happened. Grandma's very last words
before she closed her eyes were—

MARLENA. Shut the damn blinds!

GARY. Gary, just make sure of one last thing. That Dr. Franklin gets my entire Sammy Davis, Jr., collection.

skyBOY. Gary, that's racist!

GARY. It's not racist. Sammy was Jewish and he was proud of it. *(To Audience.)* Am I right or wrong? Remember, he didn't work Yom Kippur.

skyBOY. Oh yeah? Gary, what am I getting? *(To AVA.)* Watch this!

GARY. *(To JERRY.)* What should I give him, Dad?

JERRY. Give him some of the shmattas.

GARY. Grandma would have remembered how you liked to play dress up and beauty parlor with my brother Abe. I'm sure she wouldn't mind if I gave you some the housecoats and nighties from her closet—

skyBOY. All of them!

GARY. All of them.

skyBOY. Thank you.

GARY. Can we do this with some decorum?

skyBOY. I got decorum!

GARY. I don't think so. *(To VLAD.)* I'm sorry, I'll be done in a minute. I know you got some young men coming for job interviews. *(To Audience.)* One year ago I would never have been able to stand here with this kind of confidence and know that I have the strength and inner resources to get through an ordeal like this week has been. And it's only because I chose to deal with my issues with a very insightful therapist, who I'm lucky to say is my cousin Dr. Rachel Rosenbaum—

RACHEL. This is about your growth. I love you and support you, Gary.

GARY. You said something to me after the last session:

"Gary, have you noticed that every time you leave your family, you get depressed?" And it's because I don't take my power back. So I'm going to try and take it back right now for the first time by confronting my cousin Dori.

RACHEL. Good for you, Gary.

GARY. Dori, you came to Grandma's apartment last night with the maître-d' from Gargiulo's in Coney Island. We went through all seven of Grandma's photo albums. And I thought we had a very *adult* conversation. I go to the bathroom, for two seconds to make a sis, I come out and you are gone, this big Italian guy was gone, and all seven of the albums have yet to be returned. Now people are saying to me, "Gary, I want the hard boiled egg holder from the chotchke cabinet." *(To audience member.)* I know the one you want. Just give me a couple of days. "Gary, I want Grandpa Harry's prayer books and leather tefillin in the back—"

MARLENA. I just want her frequent flyer miles transferred to my account.

JERRY. Give 'em to her.

GARY. Take 'em.

MARLENA. *(Smugly.)* Thank you. I will.

GARY. They're on Tower* Air. *(*Topical, e.g., any airline on strike.)* The dreydl just turned. Grandma used to say "Der seykhl kumt shpet," the brains come late. I'm hoping they're going to come, Dori. One day, when you're a little old Jewish lady walking down the Brighton Beach boardwalk, by then I hope you'll have learned what I had the honor and privilege of learning form our Grandma this year. That it's not the chotchkes that are really important, and it's not the pearls you took out of Grandma's coffin. All we really have is each other—
(Looks back at UNCLE DAVE with his arms around RACHEL

and AVA and adds)—and a little help from Viagra. That's all we have in the end, just each other. Don't forget that, Dori.. Thank you.

VLAD. Okay, now let's all run along to the cemetery. You can get your maps...

DORI. *(She interrupts VLAD and wobbles toward GARY.)* Excuse me Vlad, I have something to say.

VLAD. Get it off your chest, Dori.

DORI. First of all, Gary it wasn't seven photo albums, it was ten! And they are mine, baby doll! And second of all, it wasn't the maître-d' from Gargiulo's, it was Javier the dish-washer from Lundy's! *(She crosses to FREDO and pulls him out of his seat.)* Come on Fredo, take me away from all this death!

FREDO. Hey, what the hell are you doing?

RISA. Fredo!

DORI. Come on Fredo, you said you were taking me to Italy!

FREDO. Sta te cit! *(Italian for shut up.)*

RISA. Fredo, if you ever want to have a baby with me, you'll get back here.

DORI. But Fredo, you promised me in the subway...

FREDO. *(Calmly.)* That's a lie, Dori, and you know it.

(FREDO sits down.)

MARK. It's okay, Dori, you can come home with me. You can sleep with the dogs.

DORI. Oh, great.

(DORI runs to skyBOY. MARK follows her. They sit together.)

GARY. Please—I don't want us to leave like this! Grandma had a tradition on our family. She would always say, "Leave with something sweet." Remember she'd wrap up a little mandel bread in wax paper for you as you walked out the door? Or she'd throw you some coffee nips! Rabbi, I'm nipless right now, but I can try to bring a little sweetness here by apologizing to my brother Todd. I'm sorry, Todd.

TODD. Oh, so you're talking to me now?

GARY. I didn't know that Dori was the one who gave you the drugs.

DORI. That's a lie!

GARY. Please, we'll deal with this later Dori, believe me we will. Remember how when you were little—we used to call him Kupi the monkey, he was such a little vants, he got into everything—and you'd always say, "Grandma, why does the statue of Moses in the lanai [or Florida Room] have horns on his head?" And she never got tired to telling you how during the time of Michelangelo there was such horrible anti-Semitism they forced him to make any Jew look like the devil. That's why the statue has horns on his head.

HARVEY. Gary, excuse me, that's incorrect.

TODD. Excuse me, Uncle Harvey, that's the story Grandma told us.

HARVEY. Yes, but it's not correct. Actually, it's a mistranslation from Hebrew to Greek to Latin. Beams of light in Greek also means horns. So when they were translating it, they translated it as horns instead of beams of light.

GARY. *(Turns to his father who is telling him to tell HARVEY to shut up.)* Uncle Harvey, what happened to you? One year ago, you were making everyone here bacon and cheddar omelets for breakfast! You know what? Next Purim you'll be a Jew for Jesus. Todd, Grandma would want you to have the statue of Moses so you never forget you're a Jew first, be proud of it...

TODD. I am.

GARY. ... and a bachelor second. Now, come give me a hug, this is how we should leave. Loving each other, arm in arm. Come with me.

TODD. Thank you. I have something I would like to say...

GARY. Forget about it. We can do it back at the house.

TODD. No, I want to say it now, Gary. Just chill out.

GARY. Go ahead, you think you're so cool.

TODD. *(From the stage.)* I have something I want to say. In front of the family and all of Grandma's friends that I, Todd Grossman, am going to do something that would make Grandma proud of me. I've found the woman of my dreams, and I'm in love and getting married.

(Everyone applauds.)

HELEN KRANTZ. Mazel Tov!

(HELEN KRANTZ holds her hands up in the air.)

TODD. I met her here today.

HELEN KRANTZ. *(Drops her arms.)* Oy!

TODD. *(Beat.)* She doesn't know it yet. *(He looks out into the audience as if he's going to pick a woman in the crowd. Then he approaches AVA and gets down on one knee.)* Ava Gerard...

UNCLE DAVE. Oy vey!

TODD. ... Will you marry me?

AVA. You must be out of your mind. I'm not your type. *(Pats his back in a brotherly way.)* Trust me. *(She looks at UNCLE DAVE and says as an aside.)* I'm getting out of here!

HARVEY. Todd, she looks like your mother!

TODD. *(AVA starts to run away from TODD, but he grabs and stops her.)* You're right, she does.

(TODD kisses AVA passionately. She pushes him to the ground.)

RACHEL. Now that's sick!

AVA. **I'M YOUR BROTHER!!!!**

JERRY. What?

AVA. I flew in from Amsterdam! *(To JERRY boldly.)* It's me, Abe. But now I'm Ava. I'm *your child*, Daddy.

JERRY. Oh no! I'm outta here.

(JERRY rejects AVA and runs away from her, NATALIE stops JERRY. TODD sprays his breath with spray.)

AVA. Daddy, don't leave me! Don't abandon me again!

GARY. *(To JERRY.)* What the hell are you running away from? Nothing changes if nothing changes! *(To AVA.)* Something's changed a little bit. It's time to start the healing!

AVA. *(To JERRY.)* You never loved me as a boy. I had hoped that maybe you could love me as a woman.

MARK. I could.

AVA. Well, I guess I was wrong. You always wanted a girl.

GARY. It's the truth!

AVA. You know, we are as sick as our secrets! And there are a lot of them here. *(She walks over to the coffin.)* I tried, Grandma...

GARY. Go to him... G-G-G-Go to her.
JERRY. How do I know that's Abe?
UNCLE DAVE. Because I paid for the operation!
GARY. Go! Be a father!

(JERRY runs to AVA to hug her.)

AVA. Daddy!

(They embrace.)

NATALIE. *(Beat.)* We got our daughter!

(NATALIE runs up to AVA and JERRY and hugs them. TODD, still a bit shocked, joins in.)

HELEN KRANTZ. Wait! Wait! Let's not forget why we're here. To honor and respect Sylvia's memory! Helga I have a tape here of Sylvia's voice, I made it in the hospital. Will you play it please?

(HELGA snatches the tape out of HELEN's hand and runs it to the tech booth.)

ELSIE. *(She gets up and helps quiet everyone.)* Yeah. Hasn't there been enough fighting? I find this very upsetting. I'm not used to all this derision.
FREDO. What?
ELSIE. Derision. I'm all alone in the world. All I have is Uncle Dave, but even though Sylvia is gone, you all got each other. So can't you come together for her sake? Thank you.

(ELSIE flops down in her chair.)

(The slide of Sylvia as a young woman with her three sons, Stanley, Jerry, and Harvey, as little boys comes up. The final recording of Sylvia Schildiner Grossman is heard.)

VOICE OVER

SYLVIA. How do we work this fakakta machine?

HELEN KRANTZ. Go ahead talk right into the microphone over there.

SYLVIA. Into the microphone? Wait a minute, let me take the cigarette out. Hello guys, this is Grandma speaking. Oh G-d! If they're listening to this, I must have died.

HELEN KRANTZ. You're not dying, Sylvia. Stop it, you're not dying.

SYLVIA. Just thinking about that makes me want to cry. Oh G-d, what is beshart is beshart. Allusinanum is nishtu by kanim. Don't forget that guys. Just love each other will ya? Just be good to each other. I want you to come to the Washington Cemetery to visit with me. I'll be listening. You can come and talk anytime. I'm not going anywhere. No more cruises, oh G-d. Kiss that new baby for me, will ya guys? I love you. I'm going to miss you. Be good to each other. Okay, I guess that's about it. Bye guys, I love you. (To HELEN a little annoyed.) *Oh, give me back that cigarette, will ya!* (Pause.) *And Helen, if Gary is still outside, will you tell him to go home and take a shower?*

(Lights up.)

MARLENA. *(Standing.)* That was a lovely Kodak moment, but since my mother-in-law, Sylvia, would I'm sure want *me*

to be the hostess of her shiva—it will be at Planet Hollywood.*
[*Or some hot, local club.]

RABBI. Marlena, no please.

MARLENA. And something incredible is coming from
Zabar's* [*or some fancy caterer], the brothers Stan and Sol
have made an incredible chopped liver mold of Sylvia's face.
There are little olives for her eyes, and you can stick a cracker
in her nose.

RABBI. Marlena please.

MARLENA. Rabbi, you don't understand...

(A verbal tug-of-war.)

RABBI. (Excitedly.) The family will be shitting Siva—

ELSIE. Rabbi! You messed up bad!

RABBI. I mean sitting Shiva at Mrs. Grosssman's house at
2540 Batchelder Street in Sheepshead Bay, Brooklyn.

MARLENA. No, Demi Moore is flipping two hundred
make-your-own Sylvia burgers right now as we speak.

RABBI. And I understand it was Sylvia's wishes to have
Natalie and Gary carry out the plans for shiva.

NATALIE. I'm sorry Marlena.

MARLENA. Feh!

(MARLENA sits down. Aside to audience member: "Who's
going to eat griebenes? It's not even on Weight Watchers."
RABBI crosses to stage. As he passes by NATALIE, she
whispers something in his ear.)

RABBI. Natalie would like everyone to know the griebenes
will be at the house this evening. Now, with the love and respect

Sylvia would want us to have for each other, and for our returning family member, I would like to call forward the pallbearers who assisted in bringing Mrs. Grossman in. The pallbearers are _____, _____, _____, and _____. Gentlemen, please come forward for Mrs. Grossman's final journey, and gentlemen, I hope you know what a great honor this is.

VLAD. Okay, so we can save a little time, if all the boys who are here for the Go-Go Boy auditions, and you know who you are, would come up on stage. Take off all your clothes, and put them in separate piles. Underwear too.

HELGA. Please! Vlad, can we just complete this service respectfully? *(To Audience member.)* You keep you clothes on!

(HARVEY and MARK walk over to the coffin. HARVEY instructs the pallbearers to lift on three. And then to wait until the RABBI is ready for them to come down.)

RABBI. And as the casket is making its way through the aisles will the immediate family, only, please follow behind it in the procession. *(To pallbearers.)* Please keep her even, gentlemen. And now with love and respect, will the mourners please rise? And if you feel so moved please join in and sing, "Oh Say Shalom." *(RABBI sings up the aisle:)*
OH SAY SHALOM BIM ROMOV
HU YA A SEA
SHALOM A LE ENU.
VA AL COL YIS RAAL
VE IM A RU, IM RU, AMEN.

(RABBI repeats until he is outside.)

VLAD. Are they gone yet? Good. I want to remind you to come back next week to the grand opening of Club Mortuary. Open bar 10:30 to 12:00. See you there. *(To D.J. booth.)* Can we have some music please?

(VLAD dances for a bit to piped-in disco music, and then leaves through the back way. HARVEY and MARLENA fight outside as the crowd disperses.)

HARVEY. Marlena, this is the last time you're going to humiliate me. You'll never shame me again as long as I live.

MARLENA. You do it all by yourself Harvey.

HARVEY. If you don't have anything nice to say, then keep your mouth shut.

MARLENA. Fine, then I won't talk to you or your family for the rest of my life.

HARVEY. You know something, Marlena? My family lives in complete harmony compared to your dysfunctional family!

MARLENA. There's not a dysfunctional bone in my family's body. You know what Harvey? I've had it with this entire Fidel Castro look of yours! I want a divorce! Is there a lawyer here? *(If no one responds she says:)* C'mon, a bunch of Jews and no lawyer? I don't buy it. Don't worry, I'll find myself a lawyer, Harvey! [*(If a lawyer does respond, she says:)* Can I have your card?]

HARVEY. You slept with my brother. You can't sleep with one brother and marry another one. That's against Jewish law. I have to give you a get, a Jewish divorce, you get the whole thing.

MARLENA. Harvey, that's what I've been asking for.

HARVEY. You know something? You remind me of my mother. My mother treated me like dreck, and you treat me like dreck.

MARLENA. Maybe you're a dreck magnet.

HARVEY. Yeah? Look what I attracted? I'm saying Kaddish. *(Over the coffin, laying on the pavement in front of the theater.)* You go where you want.

MARLENA. You can daven yourself into a coma for all I care. I'm going to Planet Hollywood* *(*local hot club.)* with _____ (an Audience member) and I'm going to order a ham and cheese on white bread with butter and mayo. And a big glass of milk. *(As HARVEY begins the Kaddish, MARLENA tells the lawyer in the audience outside:)* Honey, you start the car. I have to go make a pish. I'll be right out.

(MARLENA exits. HARVEY finishes the Kaddish and asks the remaining onlookers respectfully:)

HARVEY. What is everyone looking at?

(HARVEY exits. Because I.J. Morris hasn't sent the hearse from their competing mortuary yet, the RABBI asks MARK to guard the coffin until the hearse arrives. The RABBI reminds people to put on their headlights on the way to the cemetery. MARK passes out memorial programs. Finally, HELGA tells MARK to bring the coffin back inside and to place it between the cream cheese and the celery so that it will keep.)

sof
END OF PLAY

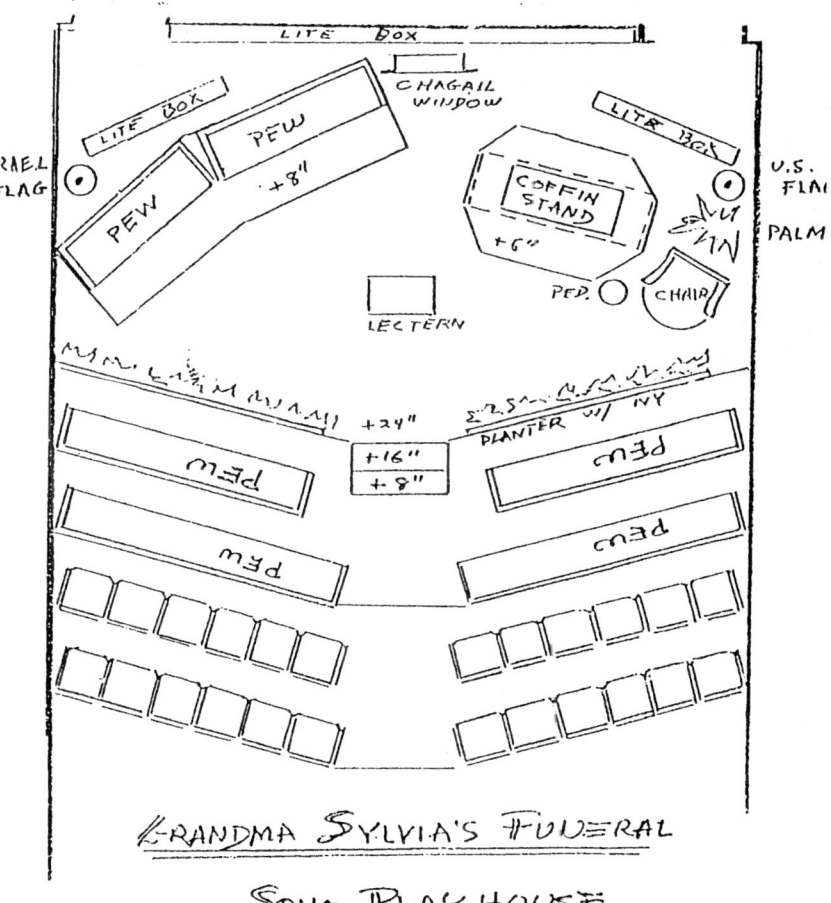

GRANDMA SYLVIA'S FUNERAL

SOHO PLAYHOUSE

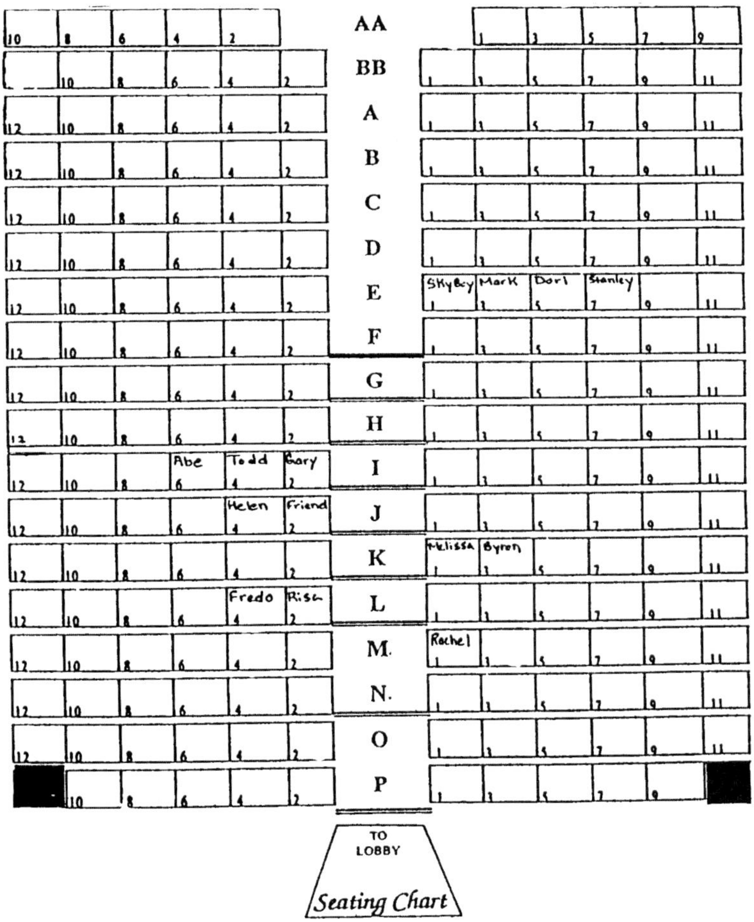
AA
BB
A
B
C
D
E
Mark
Dori
Stanley
F
G
H
I
Abe
Todd
Gary
J
Helen
Friend
K
Melissa
Byron
L
Fredo
Risa
M.
Rachel
N.
O
P
TO LOBBY
Seating Chart

HOUSE STAFF TRAINING

Grandma Sylvia's Funeral is an interactive show. That means that the audience becomes a part of the show by being treated as if they are mourners at the funeral of Sylvia Schildiner Grossman. From the moment people arrive, to the moment they leave, all crew, box office, and house staffs act as if they work for the Helsenrott Mortuary. Everyone involved becomes part of the show.

Because this is an interactive setting, some of the customary terms or ways of treating audience members have to be changed. Here is a list of words as they are, and how this show refers to them:

1. ticket = memorial card
2. auditorium/theatre = chapel
3. box office = mortuary office
4. show = funeral service
5. lobby/lounge (downstairs) = schmoozie room (during Mitzvah meal it becomes Helsenrott Bistro.)
6. theatre building = Mortuary
7. playbills/programs = memorial programs (given out at the end of the service.)
8. actors = family members
9. crew = mortuary staff
10. intermission = Mitzvah meal

Top of the Show: The basic feeling is that the crew and staff are the first people that the audience sees. We have to set the tone for the show and from the very beginning get the audience to feel as though they are attending a funeral. In order to do this effectively, we have to take the "upper hand." We have to approach them, not the other way around.

If you're on the front door, you should greet the "mourners." Say "Hello, are you here for the Grossman funeral services today?" If they say yes, give your condolences and ask if they have their memorial cards. If they don't have their cards yet, then instruct them that only one "family" member needs to go up to the mortuary office to pick them up. Unless you have a *huge* lobby, the rest of the family members can wait outside or in the schmoozie room (which can have a bar). The layout of theaters obviously varies widely.

If the audience doesn't catch on quickly, we have to help them out by getting them to realize that this is **interactive** and this is not an ordinary play. Most of them will tell you they are here for the show, we have to get them to understand that this is not a show, but Sylvia's funeral. Assure them if they are really confused (they might in fact walk away and keep looking for the theatre), that they are in the right place. You might also say that you understand that they are confused by their grief. Play with them and they will most likely play back. Do not drop the facade, unless you feel like you are in a no-win situation and the audience member will walk away, or if they are getting extremely angry.

Spatial problems will vary from theater to theater. If on the inside door, as soon as you see someone coming through the door you should greet them the same way as outside, saying, "Are you here for the funeral services?" Then follow it by saying that they need to get their memorial cards and to form a single file line going down the stairs against the wall. Many people will crowd the vestibule, and you need to instruct them that they cannot wait there because you need to keep the area clear. You might tell them that the area must be cleared so that the deceased may be brought through. If they don't form the line going down the stairs you might have to show them, or tap the wall to get them to understand where to line up. Also instruct many people that the bathrooms are downstairs in the schmoozie room.

Outside duty is to help everyone line up across the street. You need to get people to line up in pairs. You might explain that it is like Noah (lining up two by two). Your job is also to make sure no one gets run over by cars! As soon as the taxi arrives, you must keep the audience from coming into the street and keep traffic coming through.

Tearing (or taking) memorial cards, you need to keep the line moving and making sure that you get cards from everyone. Also no one is allowed in with a drink during the first part of the "services." If any problems arise with Memorial Cards, instruct anyone to talk with someone in the Mortuary Office.

If on yarmulke duty, make sure that all men get one. Tell them they have to wear one; if there's a problem, send them to the House Manager. However, the only one NOT getting a yarmulke is the actor playing Dr. Byron Franklin. Make sure that you pass him over.

Any interaction with the audience is to be solemn, quiet, polite, and respectful; but at the same time, you need to make sure to get their attention and cooperation. A good way to take command is to walk up to them directly, look them in the eye, and/or lightly touch their arm. This way we get their attention and cooperation without shouting or seeming like we are in a line at Disney World. It is amazing what you can get an audience member to do if you take the part of the "mortuary" worker seriously and let the audience play.

During the Show: We help set up for the Mitzvah Meal downstairs and also make sure the bathrooms are tidy.

During the Mitzvah Meal: We either watch the tables and refill anything that is getting low or we distribute iced tea/water. We are also responsible for keeping the lines moving and instructing people to go back upstairs once they have their plates and drinks.

Or on certain days we stand at the top of the steps (after the long hallway) to make sure no one trips and to carry plates of anyone who look like they need an extra hand. In New York, we have seen many audience members, especially older people, trip and fall. (If it looks like someone cannot handle a plate, drink, and the steps, then take their plate/drink and explain that this is part of your job. You might say that you get paid by how many plates you carry or that you are bored and need something to do. If they're approached this way, many people then will give up their plates.)

After everyone has their food and the show has resumed, we have to clean up from the Mitzvah Meal.

After the show: We need to hand out Memorial Programs to everyone as they leave. Then go into the theater and start cleaning up from the Mitzvah Meal

If it's the last show of the day, the props from outside need to be brought inside.

Information: There is certain information that the entire crew needs to know about the show. First and foremost, staff may NOT divulge any information that is scripted business in the show; this is for the actors to disseminate. If asked a question about contents in the show, simply answer that you don't know or are not sure, and that they should ask a family member or Mrs. Helsenrott when they see them. (For example, many people ask how Sylvia died, or why the Rabbi was changed.)

Here is information that we need to know about the show's environment and things a mortuary worker would certainly know.

Mrs. Helga Helsenrott (or Mrs. H.) is the owner of the mortuary. She and her son Vladimir (or Vlad) run the mortuary. They have 18 mortuary locations in the tri-state area. This is the last funeral in this location because Vlad is turning it into a dance club to be called "Club Mortuary."

The funeral today is for Sylvia Schildiner Grossman. Mrs. H. accidentally sent Sylvia to the wrong location because she doesn't know how to use the new computer system. However, mortuary workers are aware that she sent the body to the wrong location, but must simply tell people there is a short delay and we can't seat people in the "chapel" because the body is not present and this is against Jewish law. "You can't have a funeral without a coffin." *Do not tell the audience/mourners about the body being sent to the wrong location.* The crew tells the mourners that we are waiting for the hearse to arrive and that they need to line up across the street, because they can't line up in front of private residences.

Here are some questions we get and responses we give:

1. "Where are the bathrooms?"

They are downstairs. The ladies room is at the bottom of the stairs, first door on your right. Men's is in the alcove by the pay phones. (This obviously would vary from theater to theater.)

2. "Can I take my seat?"

We can't seat anyone until the casket arrives. You must wait downstairs or outside. However, there are exceptions. If someone is incapable of waiting due to infirmity, then explain that they will miss things, but we will gladly seat them. But this should be avoided. Please check with Stage Manager, House Manager, or the Asst. Stage Manager before seating anyone.

3. "Why are we waiting?"

We are waiting for the hearse to arrive.

4. "Where is the Helsenrott Gardens?"

The current sign out front says that the services are followed by the Mitzvah meal in the Helsenrott Gardens. There are no gardens; the Mitzvah meal is held in the Bistro. You can say (according to the weather) *that they have been moved inside because of the weather.* Or *they have been overrun by bugs.*

5. "What is the Mitzvah meal?"

It is a light nosh of bagels, cream cheese, lox spread, whitefish, tuna fish, veggies and dip, and iced tea. It is served about halfway through the service.

6. "How long does the show last?"
First response should be—*What show? This is a funeral service.* You can say— *Most funeral services last about 2 1/2 hours. But it really depends on the rabbi and the family.*

7. "What happened to Rabbi Freidman?"
Rabbi Freidman is the name scratched off on the memorial cards and replaced by Rabbi Wolfe. You can say, *I don't know, I was just instructed that there was a change.*

8. "Why do we have to pay to go to a funeral?"
You are not paying, you are making a donation.

9. "Are there *Playbills*?"
You can respond with—*I don't know what* Playbills *are, but I do know that a Memorial Program will be given out at the end of the service.* Never give out a *Playbill* before the end of the show.

10. "Are you part of the show?"
Again, the response should be, *What show?* Then explain that you work for the mortuary.

11. "Where is the box office?"
We don't have a box office, but if you are attending the funeral and need to pick up your memorial cards, you need to go to the mortuary office that is inside the front door of the mortuary.

12. "Where do I get my tickets?"

I don't know anything about tickets, but I know that you can get your memorial cards at the mortuary office.

13. "How long has the show been running?"

First response: *What show?* Then explain that *Mrs. Grossman just died the other day.* They may be persistent and say "How long have we been burying her?" Appear confused and again say: *She died the other day and she has only one funeral.* After this, they will usually leave you alone.

14. "What do we do when it rains/snows?"

If we have a funeral scheduled during foul weather, we have umbrellas for the rain and if it snows we proceed as always. But you can also say: *With most funerals, the body is present, and friends and family do not have to wait outside. But it is against Jewish law to enter the chapel if the body is not present.*

HAND PROPS

GENERAL

Taxi—*Depending on whether the play is being performed in a "taxi town", you should make an arrangement with a taxi company. Or use a beat up hatchback.*

Yarmulkes for audience

2 baskets for yarmulkes

Kleenex for aisles

Umbrellas for audience and characters (when raining)

1 Viewing Coffin—*There should be nothing in the coffin so it's not too heavy for the pallbearers to carry. Mark and Uncle Harvey should make sure no audience member ever opens the lid.*

3 fruit baskets (pre-set on stage)

NATALIE CHASEN

Flower for Gary after his song (pre-set on stage behind upstage pew)

Love oils

Purse

Hand necklace on a chain or rope

Kleenex (in purse)

Evian Spray mist (for face)

JERRY GROSSMAN

2 Memorial cards

Sunglasses

Yarmulke

GARY GROSSMAN

1 Memorial card

Glass of iced tea (set in podium)

Yarmulke
Kleenex (in pocket)

TODD GROSSMAN
1 Memorial card
Business cards
Marijuana cigarette (made with ginseng)
Breath spray
Lighter

RACHEL ROSENBAUM
Business cards
Briefcase
Sunglasses
Notecards
Reading glasses/eye glasses
1 Memorial card

MELISSA FRANKLIN
Musical instrument in case (violin, flute)

BYRON FRANKLIN
2 Memorial cards

RISA IANNUZZI
2 Memorial cards
Purse

FREDO IANNUZZI
Cross
Yarmulke
Rosary
Money (to give cab driver)

HELEN KRANTZ
    Bracelet (gold)
    Purse
    Hadassah pin on a necklace
    Plastic bag for bagels
    Candy (for Gary)
    Kleenex (in purse)
    1 Memorial card
    Black handkerchief
    Gold chains and earrings
    Black bobby pins (for Gary)
    Audio cassette tape (to give to Helga)

HELGA HELSENROTT
    Hanky
    Glasses on a chain
    White Yarmulke

VLAD HELSENROTT
    Cocaine bottle
    Clipboard
    Tawdry printed invitations to Club Mortuary
    Pen and Paper
    Glass (for mixed drink)
    Yarmulke
    Coat with tails

STUART "skyBOY" GROSSMAN
    Beanie with propeller (instead of yarmulke)
    Bag
    Can of yams or stuffed toy
    Wig (set in podium)

Sunglasses
1 Memorial card
Fake fur pieces
Button pins for shirt/vest/jacket

DORI GROSSMAN
Pearl necklace (set in coffin)
Sheets of paper (for the poem)
Purse
1 Memorial card
Lots of jewelry

DAVE SCHILDINER
Prayer book
cigar
Yarmulke

ELSIE DUEY
Finger nail (set on stage)
Little liquor bottle
Purse
Perfume
Toilet paper (stuck to shoe in Act II)
Lots of jewlery

MARK GROSSMAN
Pez
Pez dispenser
Broom
Dust Pan
Rubber gloves

Fantastic bottle
Yarmulke
Photos of two dogs
Small photo album
Glass (put in pocket after Mitzvah meal)
Extra yarmulkes
Diesel (little stuffed blue bear for pocket)
Paper towels

RABBI WOLFE
Glasses
Prayer book
Suit jacket (too small)
Yarmulke

MARLENA WEISS-GROSSMAN
Chewing gum
Purse
Fan (battery operated)
Water bottle
Tearaway top
1 Memorial card

AVA GERARD
Purse
Handcuffs
Lots of jewlery

HARVEY GROSSMAN
Yarmulke
2 different socks

SET PIECES

THEATRE:

In the house:

14 "reserved for family" signs in gold lettering for chairs
in the house: Dr. Rachel Rosenbaum; Risa Iannuzzi; Fredo
Iannuzzi; Dr. Byron Franklin; Melissa Franklin; Friend;
Helen Krantz; Gary Grossman; Todd Grossman; Abe
Grossman; Stuart Grossman; Dori Grossman; Mark
Grossman; Stanley Grossman (Ava's seat)

Small black boxes of Kleenex are attached to the aisle seats
of every other row

1 sign for mother poem (on wall in the back of the house
stage left):

"Mother
God took the sunshine
From the skies
And made the Lovelight
In your eyes
He gave you breath
And with his love
Made yours divine
But best of all
He made You
Mine"

On Stage:

2 "Helsenrott Jewish Mortuary" signs that have an 800
number on them (on both walls of stage)

Lights should include two "specials" on each side of the
upstage wall that flash "GARY!" at the end of his song.

Greenery (edge of stage)

2 pews (upstage right)

3 rugs (2 under pews/1 under the coffin stand)

3 platforms (2 under the pews/1 under the coffin stand)

1 Israeli flag

1 American flag

1 Chagall window

1 tag on coffin that says "$499—as is"

1 coffin stand (upstage left)

1 slide of Grandma (projected on screen stage right)

1 framed picture of Grandma (on stand stage left of coffin stand)

1 podium

1 stool

1 stand for Grandma Picture (downstage left corner of coffin stand)

1 potted fern/plant (behind Vlad's chair)

1 pillow (for Mrs. Helsenrott-downstage left corner of coffin stand)

1 wicker chair (for Vlad—downstage left corner)

4 flats (covering back walls. They are covered in lace curtains and contain strip lights)

The top step riser has the name Helsenrott in black and gold lettering

A large fruit basket by the coffin

OUTSIDE:

1 sign that lists events of the day:

(Title:) HELSENROTT MORTUARY

with stars of David on either side

On black background with white stick-in letters:

SERVICES:

Sylvia Schildiner Grossman's Funeral
Auditions for the Go-Go Boys
Announcement for the opening of Club Mortuary
with mud pits for mud wrestling

4 "No Parking Please Funeral Today" signs
1 cone for the street
1 sign (that goes in 2 hanging window display boxes on either side of the main steps listing the funeral—same as the memorial cards, and an added small sign that says: Service followed by Mitzvah Meal in Helsenrott Gardens)
1 bench
1 ash tray
1 garbage can

VESTIBULE:

1 sign (*"Welcome to Helsenrott Jewish Mortuary
Where your corpse is our concern"*)
2 Jewish Mortuary awards
2 framed letters to Helga and Meyer
21 framed awards from 1974-1996 (1986 missing)
*"The National Association of Jewish Funeral
Directors present this award to Meyer and Helga
Helsenrott of the Helsenrott Mortuary in recogni-
tion for excellence in Funeral Direction (year). Presented at the Annual Dinner of the National
Association of Jewish Funeral Directors.*
1 velvet painting

HELSENROTT BOX OFFICE:

1 sign over box office window: Helsenrott Mortuary "a
place to die for"

1 sign next to window: Helsenrott Mortuary
                        Past Date Policy
                        70 years of family tradition
1 sign below the preceeding one:
            70 years and we've never missed a Funeral
            1. All sales are final.
            2. No refunds or exchanges on Funeral Reservations.
            3. Coffins are guaranteed for one (1) year unless
                dropped.
            4. Make your Funeral arrangements in advance, for
                a place with a view.
            5. A complete private service for you and 200 of your
                friends or other group discounts can be arranged
                by calling our Group Sales Funeral Director at
                (phone number) Helsenrott.
            Dead on your feet? Lie Down and Call Us (phone #)

HELSENROTT BISTRO:
        1 concrete fountain of peeing boy (in leather outfit)
        1 sign "Helsenrott Bistro" (on reverse side reads:
            "Shmoozie Room"
        1 flat (to cover back room)
        1 coffin (made into a door for coat check)
        2 framed pictures of the Founders with brass name plates
                under each (one of Helga and one of Meyer
                Helsenrott as they were in the late 1950's)
        4-5 potted plants
        1 picture of 2 angels smoking and drinking beer
        The Helsenrott Collection (velvet paintings in elaborate gold
                frames depicting scenes from the Bible and reflect-
                ing Vlad's interest in the human body—mostly male)

RUTH	after Picasso
KING SAUL	after Jack Levine
DAVID BEN-GURION	after Dinner
MOSES & THE 10 COMMANDMENTS	after Rembrandt
MOSES & THE BURNING BUSH	after Orozco
BATHSHEBA AWAITING DAVID	after Bouche
ADAM & EVE	after Masaccio
DAVID & GOLIATH	after Roualt
DAVID	after unknown

4 notes in place of paintings (that are missing)

"This martial portrait of Marshal Moshe Dayan (47"x 57") is on semi-permanent loan to the Friendship museum in Damascus, Syria."

"This dazzling portrait of Golda Meir (35"x23") is on loan to the Ingrid Bergman Museum in Stockholm, Sweden."

"This sensitively rendered painting of Delilah trimming Samson's hair (108"x69") is one of, if not the, biggest and most impressive pictures in our collection. The black velvet had to be specially ordered in the needed width. For many years it has been a favorite among our patrons. However, with the rise of feminism and gay rights it has been deemed too ribald for a funeral chapel. It will be prominently displayed in the new Club Mortuary."

"This painting Moses and the Jews crossing the Red Sea pursued by Pharoah and the Egyptian Army (3"x 1") is the smallest painting in the Helsenrott collection. Unfortunately, it has been mislaid.

2 Helsenrott notices

"The Helsenrott Collection:

The Helsenrott Collection of black velvet is be-
lieved to be the largest collection of such art outside
of Graceland. The Helsenrotts have been accumulat-
ing this type of art since the founders developed a
fondness for it in the early 1960s, and have since
commissioned many original works by such inter-
nationally famous artists as: Gus Alicon, Gus B.
Alicon, Bert Clephne, Daphne EB, all on themes of
Jewish and Biblical history. Of course, the works of
art you see here are merely coarse copies of the valu-
able originals. The valuable originals are kept in bank
vaults and only brought out and displayed for the
services of really important persons."

15 orchestra lights

1 picture (of sexy girl signed to Vlad)

Several over the bar signs:

BAR MITZVAH	Sunrise, Sunset
Vlad's spiked cider	"The place to die for"
Scarsdale Iced Tea	"Please pardon our appearance while we're remodeling"
Shirley goes to Temple	Under Construction
Pallbearer's Punch	Coming Soon: Club Mortuary

HALLWAY:

several (gaudy, colorful) signs (Golem Go-Go Boys,
Meander Thru The Mausoleum)

2 coffin cutouts (with signs attached)
Coming Soon: Club Mortuary
Exit Signs

The Place to Die for
Dig That Body
Get Permanently Stoned
Under Construction
Mud Wrestling in the Crypt
Please Pardon Our Appearance while we're remodeling
1 wall size picture (Club Mortuary-has a picture of Moses
    holding tablets that list the following:)
Monday: Buns Contest
Tuesday: Hot Oil Wrestling
Wednesday: Smallest Briefs Wins
Thursday: Beefcake Parade
Friday: Flesh Fantasy
Saturday: A Cut Above
Sunday: Blue Boy Special
WHERE THE DEAD KEEP COMING!
Several Professional Leaflets on the walls saying:
"A place to die for"
Helsenrott Jewish Mortuary
Serving the Jewish community in New York and outlying
    areas for 40 years
Embalming while you wait
An acre of caskets to choose from
This month's special: 'Sunrise, Sunset'
Saturdays half-price. Ask about our Daily Specials."
5 Framed awards
Star Friendsh awarded to: Helsenrott Mortuary (a cut
    above the rest)
Presented by: National Foundation of Hebrew Men
November 26, 1988
Solomon Meyer   Meyer Meir
Guiss Mayer   John Majors

Funeral Direction
Awarded to Helsenrott Mortuary
Presented to Meyer and Helga Helsenrott at the formal
    presentation night at Stage Deli
Presented by Foundation of Israeli Funeral Chapels 1984
Daphne Ebb   Leon Munier
Jeff Stull

Excellence Awarded to Helsenrott Mortuary
For excellence in funeral direction by an independent
    chapel presented by
National Association 1975

Best Services 1983
Awarded to Helsenrott Mortuary
Presented by Foundation of Israeli Funeral chapels
March 5, 1983
Daphne Ebb   Leon Munier
Jeff Stull

Best Services 1988
Awarded to Helsenrott Mortuary
Presented by Foundation of Israeli Funeral Chapels
March 8, 1988
Daphne Ebb   Leon Munier
Jeff Stull

Restrooms:
 Mens:
    Black & gold Grecian-Urn Border Wallpaper
    Bas-relief of the bare back of a Roman soldier hangs
       in the stall

Signs hang on the walls that read: "The place to die for,"
"Coming soon - Club Mortuary," "Mud Wrestling in
the Crypt!"
A "Prepay" Notice is Posted
 Ladies:
Floral border Wallpaper
Several pictures of cherubs in fancy gold frames
1 picture of an old fashioned shoe with a leg
2 limoge plate hangings
A "Prepay" Notice is Posted

> Be Prepared
> Prepay
> Beat Inflation
> Do It Your Way

By SELECTING YOUR CASKET - AND THE
ACCOMPANYING SERVICE POSSIBILITIES:
 Lining Color, Flowers, Music, Number of Flower Cars,
Thank You Cards, even Gravesite - YOU CAN BE
SURE YOUR CEREMONY WILL BE AS YOU
    WANT IT.

DON'T LEAVE THESE IMPORTANT DECISIONS
TO HEIRS WHO MAY HAVE OTHER THINGS ON
THEIR MINDS.

OUR DIRECTORS WILL HELP YOU IN YOUR
DECISION.

OUR LAWYERS WILL HELP MAKE IT AIRTIGHT.

Once you Prepay and Register with us you will be entered into a World Wide Computerized Mortuary Directors Listing for ever and ever, with no additional cost to you.

So No Matter Where or When you Die, your number can be entered into any Funeral Director's (participating) Computer - and your prepaid decisions and wishes will be carried out.

In addition to you World Wide Mortuary Director's Card: you can augment your feeling of security with the purchase of a beautiful silver or gold: I.D. BRACELET, TAG OR BROOCH.

Similar to those worn by persons with special illnesses or allergies. Prices on request.

BE EVEN MORE CERTAIN
AFTER ALL
IT'S YOUR FUNERAL

NOTES FROM A WORRIED JEWISH FATHER

Bad Weather:

On rainy or sub-zero days, the audience should be taken directly into the shmoozie room. The actors should be sent to work the crowd there, doing the same business that they would perform on the line. Ten minutes before the cab arrives Natalie and Jerry should announce to the audience that Gary and Todd had to go pick up the coffin on the side of the Parkway. It would be very nice if the mourners came outside to support them. Umbrellas with the Helsenrott Mortuary emblem should be handed out.

Losing the audience:

Sometimes people will attend the funeral for reasons other than their wanting to participate in this type of theater. Some people will be offended by how the play reveals these characters, warts and all, or the family might be too much like their own and make them uncomfortable. Or they'll like the show, but not laugh much. Don't push your performance out of desperation. Play the same show you always give and if they don't come to you, too bad. Never lose the reality. The integrity of the show depends on that. Most people will love the show. But not everyone will like it. That's life.

Controlling the audience:

Sometimes there will be a large group sale where everyone has gotten drunk on the bus ride to the show. The people will be rowdier than usual. It's important that the cast set the tone for the show. The Rabbi and Mrs. Helsenrott must wait for people to quiet down. The cast should *never* be hostile to the audience. But they should play the drama more than the comedy until the audience settles down. Otherwise the audience will think the show is a big joke and they'll never come around to respecting the reality of the funeral. Once they calm down, and they usually do, then hit them over the head with all of the comedy and bring them back to a reasonable level.

Discipline:

This is an ensemble show. Actors who are upset because their part doesn't have enough laughs have no place in this type of show. Each performance is a part of the fabric and texture that make up this entire crazy quilt. Everyone is dependent on one another's generosity and dependability. You have the room to give a brilliant performance in any single part in this show, not just the ones with the most lines or the most laughs. Keep the show moving. The Rabbi, Gary, and Helga need to drive it quickly, but with varying levels that you'll all find as an ensemble with successive audiences. Being real doesn't mean being flat. Always give it the juice—the emotional commitment to high stakes.

Scripted lines, comments and asides:

A scripted line is what's in the text and usually said from the stage. A comment is a line that's meant for just a row. Your cast will find some of their own. I've tried to include some of ours. Here are a few more examples: When Melissa is walking up with Byron to do their dance, Natalie tells Risa, "First her, then you, and then me. Pregnancy comes in threes." Or when Melissa announces her son will be named Sylvio, Natalie says to Fredo, "Oh Fredo, I love the Italian!" Fredo and Byron's lines about the Q-tip and the Pope, while scripted, are comments. An aside is meant for just one or two people next to you. After Dori does her poem, skyBOY says to an audience member, "That was nice, Dori. Nice and *short.*" When Gary gives away the Chagall windows, Marlena tells the people next to her, "Knock offs!"

Nobody should be improvising lines during the presentational parts of the show. It's not fair to the people who are in the focal beat.

Beats:

Every actor should break his performance into beats no matter what kind of show he is doing. But the beats in this show must involve the focus lent to them by whatever other actors are present. Major beat means everyone lends focus, medium means some people lend focus but the beat is not presentational, and minor means a few people lend focus to a quiet moment. Example: A major beat is when the taxi pulls up. Every actor must lend focus to this. Another major beat is when Dori steals the jewelry. A medium beat is when Harvey is fighting with Helen Krantz outside on the line. Another medium beat is the fight outside between Jerry and Todd over his pot smoking. A minor beat that still needs focus is when Marlena is applying Grandma's make-up in the coffin or when Helen Krantz pats Todd's butt before the funeral and tells him that she never got around to making a man out of him after his Bar-Mitzvah and that he should come back to her place for a little noodle kugel. (She has made love to all of the Grossman men on the day of their Bar-Mitzvah.) Or when Helen begs Dave to take her back at the end of the Mitzvah meal.

Biographies and Family History:

Every actor should write a bio for his/her character that supports the text and then compare them with the other cast member's bios to make sure that all the facts are in support of each other. When new actors join the cast, they cannot create new history that conflicts with what has already been created.

What makes GSF so unique:

GSF delivers the same amount of one liners that theatergoers expect when they go to a hit comedy. At the same time, there is not one scene in this show that does not come from real life. All of these characters, every incident right down to the price tag "$499 As Is" on the coffin are from real life. Nobody can ever tell you that this show goes too far. Therefore, the performances must be real. The audiences may come expecting caricature, but they should get thought out, heartfelt, real performances. The less anger in the show, the better. No one should call anybody any bigoted names, such as nigger, faggot, shvartza, faggelah, fatso, etc. If the cast has the freedom to insult people, then the audience will feel that they have that same freedom, and this will become a mean-spirited show where people come to get stoned and rowdy. Fight for your character's integrity, and inspire people with your warmth. Remember that *Grandma* has a strong script and a nuanced structure in order for the genre to mature. Your performance should be of the same quality.

Make it your own. Have fun.

And now, in the words of my nemesis skyBOY, "I'm letting go."

Glenn Wein. Fall, 1996.

sof

Schildiner
Family Tree

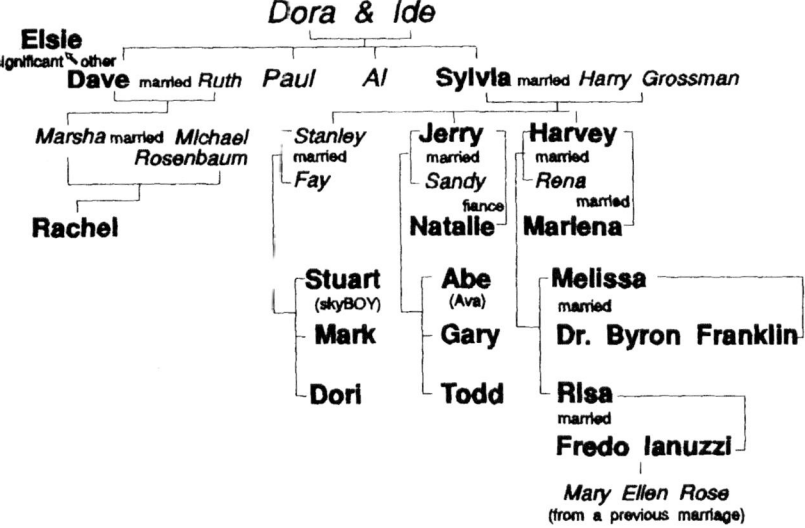

SAMPLE BIOGRAPHIES

NATALIE CHASEN

She is a true child of the 60s. She was a hooker in NY, but hardly a typical street walker. She worked on the barter system. For example, if she wanted her roof fixed, she offered her services in exchange.

She is very much into oils, chakras, meditation, auras, and "universal sexuality."

She met Jerry in 1969 when they had a brief affair before meeting again through Myra in Florida in 1970 (see Jerry bio for details).

She and Jerry are complete opposites. But this excites her about him: she loves his fire and passion. At the same time, she soothes him and has brought out his fun-loving nature.

She went to Florida in 1970 and started her love oils company. At this time she did keep "hooking" until 1975, when she started living with Jerry.

Abe did not live with Natalie and Jerry, so she doesn't know him that well. But she has strong relationships with Gary and Todd. She and Gary have good communication, and she and Todd share aspects of shopping. She is the one mother figure they had growing up. She provided the nurturing and safe environment that the boys needed.

She is a good business woman and her business is on the upswing. She is, in fact, doing better than Jerry and is the one supporting them.

ABE GROSSMAN/AVA GERARD

Abe is a transsexual who started the process 8 years ago; 4 years ago it was completed.

Abe was born in 1961. He grew up in NY until 1970, when his family moved to North Miami Beach. His parents separated in the early 1970s and he went to live with his mother, Sandy. He became the emotional nurturer for her and for his brothers.

He graduated high school in 1978 and joined the Marines.

Eight years ago, he started the process to become Ava Gerard. Gerard is the French word for Gerald (where Jerry's name derives from). She is a combination of her two parents, Jerry's mannerisms, and Sandy's personality.

Ava lives in Amsterdam and NY, though she spends most of her time in NY. She has two shops called "Head and Neck" (hats and scarves), one in Manhattan at 55th and 7th and one in Amsterdam. She is not that wild and is very sophisticated.

She was Dori's OA sponsor to get information about her family. Dori thinks Ava is Jerry's illegitimate daughter (see Dori's bio for details). They had a lesbian affair.

She loves her brothers and is protective of them, but she is also disappointed in them. The only family member who knows about her is Dave. He paid for her operation and for the last several years she has met with him once a week for coffee to get news of the family. Eventually, Sylvia found out, and she told Helen Krantz. She has had contact only with Dave, and this was more out of need for money than love.

JERRY GROSSMAN

Has been engaged to Natalie Chasen for 14 years, though he is still married to his wife Sandy, who is in a mental hospital in Florida. He is too guilty and it is too much trouble to go for the Get from Sandy. He is also not sure he wants to get married again.

He and Natalie are trying to have a daughter. Jerry is mostly doing this for Natalie; he is unsure if he wants to have any other children.

Jerry was born in 1936. He grew up in Queens before the family relocated to Sheepshead Bay, where he went to Sheepshead Bay High. From there, he joined the Marines. Sometime before 1960, he met Sandy and married her. She has lots of family money.

He was a cop from 1962-1970 at the 115th precinct in Queens. He knows lots of players in town and is friendly with them, but he did no deals with them. It was also during this period that Jerry had a one-night stand with Marlena. In 1970, he left NY and went to Florida (N. Miami Beach).

He actually met Natalie twice, once in NY in 1969 where they had a brief affair and again in Florida. In Florida they were set up on a "blind" date by Myra who worked security at the Miami Intl. Airport. Natalie brought out the humor in Jerry. During that first date they played a joke on Myra: they called her up and told her that they had gotten married.

Jerry went into the security business with a partner who was a former narcotics detective and ex-convict.

Jerry has three sons: Abe, Gary, and Todd. When Sandy and Jerry separated in the early 1970s, Abe went to live with his mother and Gary and Todd stayed with Jerry. In 1978, Sandy voluntarily put herself in a mental institution. Jerry has never visited her there; family money provides for her.

1978 is also the year that Jerry last heard from Abe. Jerry was embarrassed by Abe and was never close to him. Jerry has made no effort to contact his son since 1978.

Jerry is most like Uncle Dave. He has had lots of women,

and he and Natalie have an open relationship. He does have a violent temper. He did hit his boys, the way his father Harry did when he was growing up. Natalie has calmed his temper and has brought out his gentler side.

He thinks he has a good relationship with Gary and Todd, and thinks he is close to them. But in reality they merely tolerate him; he is not very sensitive.

He can't stand Uncle Dave or his brother Stanley. Jerry is the most shmoozie and personable of Sylvia's children and the one most there for Sylvia. He is Helen Krantz's favorite.

Jerry's business in Florida is on the decline, and when Harvey asks Jerry for a job, Jerry makes up an excuse to turn him down. He does not tell him the real reason is that his business is going kaput. Ironically, Natalie's business is flourishing and she is the bread winner at the moment.

This is his first time returning to NY, and he is under a lot of pressure. He has bad memories of NY and can't wait to leave.

TODD GROSSMAN

Born in 1970 in Miami. His parents separated a few years later and the person he most remembers as a mother is Natalie.

He went to North Miami Beach Senior High School and has moved out to LA, where he works for *The Tonight Show.*

He is a womanizer and party man like his father.

The reason for the marriage proposal is that everyone around him is getting married and he wants to show everyone how grown up he is. He loves his brother Gary, but he does tend to get on his nerves. His father is always on his case about the women and drugs.

GARY GROSSMAN

Was born in 1966 in NY.

Of this next generation, he is the one that people are going to be most dependent on. He thrives on co-dependent relationships.

He is most like his mother Sandy. He is an unsuccessful singer. After the funeral, he will go back to Miami and flounder again in college.

He tolerates his father, but is not very close to him. Gary got a job from his father (prior to moving to NY to care for Sylvia) as a security guard on the night shift at British Airways. At night, he would sing on the runway.

Of any family member, Gary knows that after the funeral and shiva the family will never be together again, because Sylvia kept the family together.

HELEN KRANTZ

In her 70s. Sylvia was Helen's mother's friend. She became like a "little" sister to Sylvia. Because she did not have much of a family, she built her life around Sylvia's.

She had relationships with Dave in the early 1920s before he met his wife Ruth. She has always been in love with him. She married Larry Krantz on the rebound. Larry was a sailor and went into the war. They grew apart and Helen went to work at the local community center where she later became a director of the center. Larry was a closeted homosexual and died from a heart attack in another sailor's bed Sylvia contacted the Helsenrott Mortuaries (run by the first Helga), who helped cover up how Larry died so there would not be a scandal. Helen was relieved by his death because it meant no divorce.

Sylvia and Helen became confidantes (especially after

Harry died), and Helen moved into the apartment next door in Sheepshead Bay. At this time, Sylvia and Helen started traveling together on trips that Dave underwrote.

Helen has slept with Dave and his brothers. She was known to be "passed" around. She then extended her "services" to all the Grossman men on the eve of their Bar Mitzvahs; she has become a family tradition. She did miss Todd, though, because she was in California at the time of his Bar Mitzvah. (She sleeps with all these boys because she feels obligated to teach them all safe sex.) She has now extended her services to the Hebrew School which has gotten her into trouble with the Hadassah Girls, who practice next door.

She and Sylvia are members of the Hadassah. She met Helga (the second) while they were all members. Sylvia and Helen formed the Hadassah Girls chorus. Sylvia was instrumental in getting members to join because she was so popular. She became the first president and held office for four terms. Helen became the second president, but her election was clouded in controversy (there was a demand for a recount). She has been recently forced to resign because she has sex with the boys at the Hebrew School and because of the money she "borrowed." She will tell anyone she took the money to buy music and she intends to pay it back.

She is treated like one of the family, and she attends all family functions. She is fun-loving and is the yenta for the older crowd. She knows about Risa's abortion and knows about Abe's surgery because Sylvia told her in the hospital.

DORI GROSSMAN
30 years old. (See skyBOY Bio for details about Mother and Father). Mother died when she was 5 years old.

She went to Dewey for her GED. Many family members are constantly giving her money. Rachel has given her money for her drug rehab, but Dori spent it on drugs.

She cannot hold a job, but Vlad has promised her a job in his club.

She met Elsie and Marlena when she was shoplifting at Alexander's.

She knows Ava because Ava was her OA sponsor. After a meeting one day, Dori was looking through Ava's wallet and saw a picture of Jerry. Ava told her she was Jerry's illegitimate daughter. Dori does not know Ava is Abe.

Dori has many boyfriends.

Dori was smart in school, but she stopped applying herself and put on the dumb persona because it gets her what she wants. She is very sly and manipulative.

STUART skyBOY GROSSMAN

31 years old. Mother died when he was 6 years old. His mother was at Coney Island Hospital for pneumonia. She was taking a shower unattended when she slipped, hit her head, and died. It was ruled an accident. He blames Uncle Dave for her death because he felt Dave should have moved her to a better hospital (Dave was paying for her stay). Because of this death, Sylvia gave these children (Dori, Mark, and Stuart) the most attention.

His father, Stanley, brought up the family in Brooklyn. Later they moved to Midwood. Stanley lives currently with his new wife (Gloria) and her son (who was just Bar Mitzvahed) in Postenkill, on his asparagus farm. Stanley is college educated and does not get along with Jerry or Harvey. He is described as boring and mild-mannered.

Stuart went to the University of Utah. Sylvia was pressuring him to go into medicine. This led to a nervous breakdown. To alleviate his stress, he also took some acid and had a bad "trip". He dropped out of school and returned to Brooklyn to live with Dori.

Marlena has also taken these kids under her wing and currently fronts his performance art. Marlena and Dori are the only family members he gets along with.

He currently lives at 121 Central Ave., Staten Island, in an apartment.

skyBOY's perception of Sylvia is that of a meddlesome and mean person.

He has a side job as a clown for birthday parties, but he denies this if asked about it.

At Melissa's wedding he did a piece of performance art where he took off his clothes and did obscene things with candied yams.

He has seen and talked with Vlad at the clubs in town, but the funeral today is the first time they hook up and flirt with each other.

MARK GROSSMAN

Is 28 years old. His Mother died when he was 3 (see skyBOY's Bio for details).

He lives in an apartment paid for by his father in Brighton Beach a block from where Sylvia lived as a young woman. (See skyBOY's bio for details about his Father.)

He used to work for the Park's Dept. and now lives off of a disability check. He picks up extra part-time work at the mortuary for $1.59/hour; Sylvia got him the job.

He also had a job at a convenience store, but it was held up and the burglars took Mark for a ride and he has never been the same since.

Mark is not retarded. He is only slow and neglected. He got little attention growing up and has not developed much past the age of 12.

He has a girlfriend named Bernadette who also attends "special" classes with him.

FREDO IANNUZZI

Italian Catholic. Married to Risa for 5 years, this is his second marriage. (His age is flexible.)

He grew up in the Bronx (this can be slightly changed for the actor) and that is where his marble business is located. He is NOT in the Mafia, but is well connected.

His family does not like the Grossmans and they don't interact with them much. He has one daughter, Mary Elena Rose, who lives in Italy with her mother.

Having an affair with Dori. Close with Marlena.

MARLENA WEISS-GROSSMAN

In her 40s. She is the black sheep of her family. She is one of three children. She dropped out of college in the first year and went to the Wilford Beauty School.

She met Jerry when she was 19 years old and they had a one time sexual experience at Coney Island. She secretly fell for him, but he did not return the feeling.

She met Dori when Dori was shoplifting at Alexander's, where Marlena worked doing makeovers. Dori introduced her to Harvey 10 years ago. She thought he was a nice Jewish man who didn't treat her badly like all the other men in her life. She married him 2 years later.

She got an Asst. Makeup job on Broadway through doing the makeovers (in a converted bathroom) at Alexander's. She then convinced Harvey to move to L.A., where she started doing her movie makeup work.

It was at this time that Harvey became ultra religious.

She thinks Risa and Melissa are spoiled JAPs. She has taken skyBOY, Mark, and Dori under her wing. She also gets along with her stepdaughters' husbands.

Has a NY home at 85th and Columbus that she sublets to whomever is the current big Broadway star. Ex.: Glenn Close in *Sunset Boulevard*. She's right and everyone else is wrong all the time.

HARVEY GROSSMAN

Is a former hippie who married young (Rena) and got divorced 13 years ago.

He was a former Air Traffic Controller who went on disability 7 1/2 years ago. He gets migraine headaches from Marlena but thinks they're from when he was an air-traffic controller.

He married Marlena 8 years ago, and has recently become ultra-religious.

HELGA HELSENROTT

Born in a small country not heard from much since the Iron Curtain fell, Kraplachia. She lived for many years all over Eastern Europe. Met Meyer and they settled in NY. (If the actress is young: She and Meyer took over the Helsenrott Mortuaries from his mother who was also named Helga. Helga the first had only one mortuary location, the one in SoHo.)

Meyer recently died in a shower accident, and though Helga

suspects Vlad of wrongdoing, she tells no one of her suspicions.

She lives part time in Brighton Beach, but also has an apartment over the funeral home that she shares with Vlad.

She has known Sylvia and Helen for over 20 years. She is a member of the Hadassah Girls and became friends with Helen first.

MELISSA FRANKLIN

Lives in Manhattan with her husband of 3 months, Byron Franklin. She met him in court.

She went to Yale on scholarship and is an ACLU lawyer.

She has a bad relationship with her stepmother, Marlena. She used to be close to her father, Harvey, before he became so religious. Her mother (Rena) and her father divorced 13 years ago. Rena has moved to Paris with her gynecologist, though Melissa and her sister were told by her father that it was her "foot" doctor. Her parents married young and Harvey is a former hippie.

She is one year younger than Risa. She knows about Risa's abortion.

BYRON FRANKLIN

Grew up in Brooklyn and went to Columbia University. Originally on a basketball scholarship, Byron hoped to go professional, but an ankle injury sidelined him and he took up medicine.

Met Melissa a year ago in court. She was representing a rape victim and he was called as a witness because he was the emergency room attendant.

RISA IANNUZZI

Is her mother's daughter. (See Melissa Bio for information about Mother and Father.) She currently lives in West Hartford, Connecticut, with her husband of 5 years, Fredo.

She spent 3 months at an eating disorder clinic for bulimia. Had an abortion (it was Fredo's) prior to that stay because she was worried about getting fat. Fredo is not aware of the abortion, but Melissa, Rachel, Sylvia, Helen, and Dave know.

She is aware of Dori's crush on Fredo and knows something is going on, but does not know the extent of it.

RACHEL ROSENBAUM

Her parents, Marsha and Michael, are not at the funeral because they have not been in communication with Rachel since her book came out. Marsha is the strong person in that relationship; Michael is a coward. Her parents live in West Palm Beach.

Rachel lives bi-coastally, with apartments in both L.A. and New York. She just flew into NY for the funeral and is staying at the Waldorf-Astoria. She sublets her NY apartment.

She spent her early youth in Michigan (this can change with the actor playing the role). Later she and her parents moved to Miami, where her parents hooked up with Gary's family.

Dave not only paid for Rachel's father's business, but also her undergraduate schooling at Hunter College. She has tried to pay him back and sends him checks (but he won't cash them).

She went on to LaGuardia Community College where she received her honorary degree in Psychology and Sociological studies with a specialty in spankology. She is not a true doctor and is mostly hype (talk show psychologist). She is the yenta for the younger audience members.

She has a strong relationship to Melissa.

She, too, knows about Risa's abortion. She is bisexual.

RABBI MICHAEL WOLFE

Has known Sylvia a long time because she was at his Bar Mitzvah. His mother has known Helen and Helga for many years. His parents are divorced and his mother is making her way across the country in a Winnebago.

He grew up with Risa, Dori, Melissa, and Harvey. He also went to Hebrew school with Vlad. None of them recognizes him now because he moved to Chicago 15 years ago. His father has a synagogue there.

He was a minor league baseball player before going to school to become a Rabbi.

His first 3 years of Hebrew College were in Chicago. He recently moved back to New York where he is a fourth year student at Hebrew Union. He lives near the school at 4th St. between 2nd and 3rd.

VLADIMIR HELSENROTT

Recently (last few months) moved back to NY from Romania, where he was sent to learn the mortuary business. He is in his early 30s.

His father, Meyer, died mysteriously a few weeks after his return. Though not known to anyone (Helga suspects), he killed his father by hitting him on the head with a bag full of marbles while his father was taking a shower. It was ruled an accident because it looked like he slipped in the shower and hit his head.

He lives with his mother over the funeral home.

He knows many of the Grossman children. He was a problem child known for torturing birds and other animals in the neighborhood. He sees skyBOY at the gay clubs and at the funeral today is the first time they "hook up."

He is aggressively taking over the business.

ELSIE DUEY

Has been with Dave Schildiner for 6 years. She lives with him in an apartment on the Upper West Side at 71st and Broadway.

She came into the family through Dori. Years ago, she was working with Marlena at Alexander's, where Elsie sold jewelry and Marlena was doing makeovers. One day Dori was caught shoplifting. Instead of turning her in, they took her under their wing. Dori then introduced Elsie to her Uncle Dave.

Elsie does not get along with Dave's granddaughter, Rachel, because of Elsie's drinking problem. Rachel does not approve.

Elsie had a close relationship to Dave's sister, Sylvia. They were friendly, but theirs was a rivalry there for Dave's affection.

Elsie does have a problem with drinking. But she is a "happy" drunk and is a positive, smart character. She does not make bitchy choices. She is not a villain; she likes/loves everyone.

DAVE SCHILDINER

Is Sylvia's baby brother; she was like a second mother to him growing up. They had a very close relationship that almost bordered on incestuous. She (and his mother) are the two great "loves" of his life.

He had two older brothers, Paul and Al. Paul was a taxi driver and Al was a bookie. They are deceased.

Dave has invested in real estate. He invested in Carnarsie long ago when it was cheap, and he now owns half of it. He has a condo in Carnarsie at Remsen St. (between Ave. N and Seaview Ave.) in the development of Ocean Park Condos (fictitious). He lives with Elsie at 71st and Broadway in an apartment.

His wife is dead. They did not have a great marriage. She was mentally ill, though she was never hospitalized. She lived in Florida while he lived in New York. But he took care of her until she died.

He was introduced to Elsie 6 years ago through Dori.

His daughter is Marsha (Rachel's Mother). He does not have a strong tie with her because while she was growing up he was away on business.

He had a brief relationship with Helen Krantz in the late 1930s.

He has also known Helga since their childhood.

He is a philanderer.

He bankrolled Ava's operation, Rachel's schooling, Michael's business (Rachel's father), and Sylvia's vacations. He gives money to a lot of the family, but he also finds the cheapest way to do this. He paid for skyBOY's mother's hospital stay at Coney Island Hospital, where she died in a hospital accident. skyBOY blames him for her death because he feels Dave should have moved her to a nicer hospital. He also paid for Risa's abortion.

THE WRITING ON THE WALL ABOUT
INTERACTIVE THEATRE
by Glenn Wein
5/26/96

As one of the co-creators of "Grandma Sylvia's Funeral" I often am made to feel like a forerunner of jazz. If I don't play in a Harlem speakeasy, it's not jazz. Our show is often compared to "Tony n' Tina's Wedding," (the Scott Joplin of interactive theatre) and, at first, this bothered me. Then I accepted that people were searching for some reference points to guide them in a relatively new form of theatre, which, in New York at least, is still all the rage. In a way I couldn't really blame them. Aside from "Tony n' Tina's," there really wasn't much to compare our show to.

More recently, as we entered out 18th month in New York at the SoHo Playhouse, I began to feel that the comparisons were coming less and less. Our audiences were becoming more interactive-literate (to use an apt term) and they were coming to "Grandma Sylvia's Funeral" ready and eager to plumb the possibilities of interactive theatre. We'd become the Jelly Roll Morton of the movement.

While interactive and environmental theatre projects are gaining in popularity in many cities, it's interesting to note the increasing popularity of interactivity in many other areas of entertainment. Is there a connection? Does the interest in interactive theatre parallel a similar interest in the areas of computers, the Internet, and other electronic media? Are we looking more for connection wherever we can find them as we are becoming more and more detached?

These are some of the things people discuss when they experience interactive theatre. Playwrights, as a class, might have other agendas in their conversations. They may feel, from what they've heard and seen, that interactive theatre devalues text and the act of "story writing." I've heard this argument, but I've challenged any naysayer to read the text of "Grandma Sylvia's Funeral" and see how carefully scripted all the proceedings actually are. And how, as in any theatrical production, the author (or authors) play a decisively vital role.

In fact, a lot of the improv we do can be viewed as scripted. In the case of our improvising with the audience, our actors, who bring a lot of family history to their parts, may say the same things night after night, but since we're saying them to different people with different people with different results, they are forced to reinvent their reactions to dramatic situations every time they do them. It is truly scripted improv. As the director, and because I act in the company, I am constantly playing with the material we've developed as an ensemble— as would any playwright working closely with a director and the actors. We choose what works, what resonates, then we fix it in place.

Theatre purists praise their art form in terms of how the audience is different every night, and how the chemistry is different every night, and how theatre can actually be dangerous because of this. Interactive theatre takes this premise to an extreme. It makes the connection between audience member and actor not only tangible across the footlights, but tangible in every other way. To be crude, the point is you can actually go to the bathroom with a character in an interactive play. You're talking to them, they're talking to you, you're standing over a sink, unburdening yourself, shedding your illusions ... Whatever it is, we encourage this Freudian honesty.

After an actor has worked in interactive theatre, when he goes back to work with a fourth wall, it feels like making love with a condom on. The danger and feeling of closeness have been diminished.

In interactive theatre we acknowledge that the audience is a character in the play. In "Grandma Sylvia's Funeral" we accept them as mourners at the funeral of a wonderful family matriarch, Sylvia Schildiner Grossman, and we encourage them to take on this identity, through the process of participating in a ritual which happens before them. Sometimes the audience will interrupt an actor in order to get a piece of information they wouldn't have gotten if they remained passive. When the focus is on the audience almost as much as the text, the audience's response takes on greater meaning and impact. The actors therefore have the freedom to comment on the way the audience is responding, in order to make things seem more real, and in order to take their power back from a bad audience or to ride the wave of a smart one. It really takes the actor/audience alchemy to a new level of virtual conspiracy.

Actors are placed everywhere throughout the theatre. There is no real caste system of first, second, and third class seats in interactive theatre. It's very nature is communal and inclusive. Smart interactive actors do not accost audience members who want to be left alone. When an audience member telegraphs an "I'm above this" attitude, the actor mirrors this "performance" as much as the audience traditionally mirrors an actor's output. This leads to many brief and intense relationships, which add up substantially in the course of the performance. A lot of entertaining communications, that were never scripted and never intended to be, result from this arrangement. Does that mean these communications between people are any less literary than a play scenario arising from the mind of one, solitary playwright? I wouldn't rush so quickly to judgment.

People actually become unusually proprietary about inter-active plays. It's their show, it's their family. There are people crying in the audience and you can comfort them, or you can cry and someone is bound to hug you. It almost becomes a form of therapy in addition to entertainment. There's some-thing very cathartic about it, as all art strives to be. When the character Aunt Marlena insults you at the funeral, you can answer her back in a way that you may not be able to talk to your real aunt. You've responded as you'd expect yourself to, as you'd expect any sensible person (including a fictional char-acter) to react. But because it is a place of virtual reality, the censure you feel is not real and you tend to brush it off. Sud-denly having Aunt Marlena answer you back with expletives and insults triggers you to get in touch with your inner rage and stand up for yourself for the first time. Having it happen in the public space of "the family funeral" is like a shot of primal therapy.

Again, is it any less literary if, each night, we hear a group's story together as opposed to the imaginings of a single author?

Our audiences feel that it was *their* story that got told that night, that *they* were implicated in the dilemmas of this unusually colorful, mostly Jewish family. Parts of their own biography made it into the complex tapestry of feelings that is a funeral ceremony. It was inevitable. They were one of the more than 200 "authors" of "Grandma Sylvia's Funeral" that night. And they would go home with that rare sense of pride that comes with authorship.

Many of our audience members have taken this sense of proprietariness about the show to new levels. We've had an older woman swipe a ring from Aunt Marlena, claiming she deserved it, and that everyone in the family (wrongly, she said) didn't want her to get anything. I've heard that people like to see how their boyfriends or girlfriends will "act" in the family setting of our show, almost as a kind of virtual trial-run, "to see if they can handle *my* family." People have come up to me and said they were grateful our show allowed them to confront emotions they had repressed at the funerals of actual loved ones. The experience got them to feel closer to these loved ones. Sometimes closer than they'd felt since losing them. It also helped them to laugh in the face of death.

We have the chance in interactive theatre to harness the energy between creator and creative consumer, to tell our stories truthfully and evocatively. We can tell the stories of our times, and even preach without anybody noticing. But we have to be willing to accept it all, no matter which minority or social outcast we may be related to. We all fit in.

If we don't have faith in this collective story, or the courage to confront the many demons that may surround it, we should go back to the inner sanctum of the proscenium theatre and sit in the dark waiting for the musing of those lone writers.

In the meantime, interactive theatre gives us a platform to show gesture and deed as separate from words, and just as powerful. We become adept at handling all the stories—those invented and those that are part of the text. And we embrace everything around us, the Jews, the gentiles, the blacks, the gays, the addicts, the depressed, and the self-actualized. Nobody escapes our obsessive "love."

"Grandma Sylvia's Funeral" is not necessarily a political statement, but a statement about families that is political. If we *do* want to confront who we are, warts and all, it can be done in the open, with less pretense, on the street or in the restroom, as well as on stage. The playwright becomes the conscience of the actors, driving them to meet each and every one of us, half way or all-the-way. It's *very* unsafe theatre with safe and healthy consequences.

—As published in *The Dramatists Guild Quarterly*
(Fall 1996)